Answers Without Questions

Conversations about Writing and Creativity

Answers Without Questions

Conversations about Writing and Creativity

Lowell Mick White

ALAMO BAY PRESS
SEADRIFT•AUSTIN

Copyright © 2024 by Lowell Mick White

All rights reserved. No part of this book may be reproduced in any form without permission in writing from the publisher, except by a reviewer who may quote brief passages in a review.

Cover Art: *"Georgia O'Keeffe, Hands and Horse Skull"* by Alfred Steiglitz. Art Institute of Chicago
Author Photograph: LMW
Book Design: BTP

For orders and information:
Alamo Bay Press
Pamela Booton, Director
825 W 11th Ste 114
Austin, Texas 78701
pam@alamobaypress.com
www.alamobaypress.com

Names: White, Lowell Mick, 1958- author.

Title: Answers without questions / Lowell Mick White.

Description: Austin [Texas] : Alamo Bay Press, [2024] | Includes bibliographical references.

Identifiers: ISBN: 978-1-943306-24-4 (paperback) | LCCN: 2023943423

Subjects: LCSH: Creative writing. | Fiction--Authorship. | Creative ability. | Dialogue. | Setting (Literature) | Language and languages in literature. | Time management. | LCGFT: Essays. | BISAC: LANGUAGE ARTS & DISCIPLINES / Writing / Fiction Writing. | EDUCATION / Essays.

Classification: LCC: PN145 .W55 2024 | DDC: 808.02--dc23

For
Florence Davies

It is time for writers to admit that nothing in this world makes sense.
    —Anton Chekhov

The writer is an explorer.
    —Ralph Waldo Emerson

Answers Without Questions

Introduction: About *Answers Without Questions*   xiii

1. Be Patient with Yourself   1
2. You Can Do a Lot with Human Emotions   5
3. Like Everything Else, it Will Come with Practice   9
4. So Much of What is Considered Success is Luck   13
5. Guilt Won't Get Your Book Written   17
6. Just Keep Going Down One Path or Another   21
7. We Are All Complicated   27
8. Cultivate Humility and Patience   30
9. Just Put Down Words One After Another....   34
10. Experimenting is Part of the Process   38
11. Knowledge is Good   42
12. Try Pushing Ahead   46
13. Happy Endings Should Be Earned   50
14. You're Writing About People   53
15. Your Characters are Hungry   57
16. Being Influenced is a Good Thing   60
17. All Your Ideas Have Potential   64
18. It's All Things You Can Learn   67
19. Your Heart is Original   71
20. Dodge Around the Internal Editor   74

21. How a Text Means, Not What a Text Means	78
22. Write for Yourself	81
23. What You're Writing is Good Enough	84
24. Rehabilitate Your Darlings!	88
25. Don't Give Up So Easily	92
26. You Will Fix the Flaws in Revision	96
27. Make Your Characters Half Crazy and Wholly Odd	100
28. There is Always a Way to Write Something....	103
29. Surprise is a Very Low Level of Discourse	106
30. Everything Gets Better with Practice	110
31. Lower Your Standards	113
32. Just Be Kind	117
33. Your True Self	121
34. Don't Be Safe	125
35. It's Better Just to Fix the Flaws	128
36. Political is Good	132
37. Don't Make the Reader Do the Writer's Work	136
38. No More Cheesy than You Want it to Be	140
39. Write Banned Books	144
40. Choose by What's in Your Heart	148
41. Some People are Going to Hate Your Writing	152
42. Make the Story Better	156
43. Read and Understand the World	160
44. Daylight's Burning	163
Reading List	167
Acknowledgments	179
About Lowell Mick White	181

Answers Without Questions

Introduction
About *Answers Without Questions*

YEARS AND YEARS AGO, WHEN I WAS A BLOCKHEADED GRAD student, I was teaching a composition class and I put together a super-complicated essay prompt and presented it to the students. They just sort of stared at me. I asked if they had any questions.

There were no questions.

That was absurd. I mean, I wrote the stupid prompt, and *I* had questions! There had to be questions. So I had the students write down whatever questions they had about the assignment, and pass their questions to the front of the classroom.

And it turned out that, yeah, they had some questions—very useful questions that they were apparently too shy or intimidated to ask orally.

*
**

Like just about all schools, my university shut down for the virus in March 2020, and after spring break we brought our classes back on Zoom.

I'd never taught a class on Zoom before—had never even

been on it until I'd had a pandemic happy hour chat with a friend the week before classes resumed. I was faced with the interesting and somewhat anxiety-inducing problem of holding a creative writing class in this new environment, and after pondering on it for a bit, I decided that questions were the solution. Written questions, and answers.

After the composition class years ago, I'd continued doing this in my literature classes as a way of getting discussions going, and it seemed to work. Maybe it would work even better with creative writing on Zoom! So I got on our Learning Management System—we were still using Blackboard then—and I set up a weekly discussion assignment and called the assignment a Participation Question. I posed the prompt:

Please ask a serious question about the readings or about writing or about the class....

The questions were due early in the week, and students would write and post their questions. Then I'd write out answers, and in the Wednesday or Thursday Zoom classes I'd go over questions and the answers and elaborate if necessary and tell stories and try to be profound.

That's the origin of this book. *Answers Without Questions* is the result of four long semesters and a couple of summer sessions—14 or so classes, mostly entry-level creative writing classes but with an advanced fiction class and few lit classes mixed in, with enrollments ranging from 15 to 40 students per class.

These are the answers I gave to the questions. But the questions themselves...I got rid of them. For one thing, I didn't have the permission of all the young scholars to use their writing/questions. For another...the lack of context in the answers adds a level of mystery and ambiguity, at least to me.

You will definitely notice some repetition in my answers. That's because, over the course of two years, many questions got asked more than once. Sometimes many times more than once. I've just tried to stay more or less consistent in my answers.

※

One of the sad repetitions you'll find here is the Shelby Hearon "never the book in your head" anecdote. Shelby was a novelist and was my first creative teacher back in spring semester, 1979. Our class was called "Regional Writers," and was offered not by the English Department but by the American Studies Department. I was a bone-stupid kid and didn't know what to expect. We met in a seminar room on the third floor of Garrison Hall at the University of Texas, and the moment Shelby entered the room and sat down at the head of the table and opened her mouth, I was—changed.

Awhile back, doing some post-pandemic cleaning and sorting, I came across one of my notebooks from that time. On one page I wrote

It's never the book in your head!

Shelby said that. (Not in class, actually. My memory is that we were in an elevator over at the Ransom Center, going to see a speaker). And she repeated, emphasized the word "Never." I remembered this and wrote it in my notebook because what she said made perfect sense to me, then and now—that the book (story, poem, essay, whatever) exists perfect and pristine in the safety of your brain, but by the time it's miraculously transformed into physical existence, it's become something *different*. There's no predicting whether the final creative artifact will be better or worse than the one in your head, but you can guarantee that it'll be different.

※

So, anyway, to return to and apply Shelby's Wisdom: this is not the book that was in my head when I was thinking about a book. But it is the book that came out of my fingers into a keyboard and computer, and eventually onto some paper, and that will have to be enough. It's a sort of record of some of the things we did and do in my creative writing classes, and on that level it might be useful.

LMW

1.
Be Patient with Yourself

WE LIVE IN A WORLD WHERE ALL THE STORIES HAVE BEEN written except the one you're about to write.

You're a young writer, so I would advise you to try different things, to try different methods, to not overthink the perfect balance, to spend time discovering how you see the world and finding out what works for you right now....

Plot is probably just not that important at this point. Writing is what is important. And most short stories do not have rising action, etc. Though things *happen*.

Six to eight pages is a very compact narrative space.

That said, you can do a lot in six pages....

Maybe start by making a more-or-less usable outline before you write? It's good to know where you're starting from....

Character and setting are both more important than plot. Come up with them first.

Name the place. Always (almost always?) name the place.

Examine your surroundings. Use Google streets. And Google in general. Creative writers do research!

This might sound sarcastic, but I'm totally serious: try writing a relationship story about two people who are not attractive and sparkly but are (like most of us) clunky and awkward. Things don't have to work out for them!

Observe your friends who are in relationships—what do they do? How do they behave? Use that material.

You're writing a story, not an idea. Nobody wants to read a concept.

Me, I go with a lot of dialogue—probably too much dialogue. But then I will slow things down with more exposition.

The best book I've ever read on writing is *The Midnight Disease*, by Alice Flaherty.

I keep going hard because I know I won't live long enough to tell all the stories I know. Got to get them on the page while I can.

But also look at the stories we read—they are all fine.

Those weird dialogue commas are annoying but necessary (unless you're Cormac McCarthy).

You don't have to worry about those when you write an essay...mostly...which is why they seem weird when you suddenly start writing fiction.

You can learn this. It just takes practice....

Me—sure, I'm an oddball. I'm a writer.

My job is to bear witness to the world I was born into. I have to pay attention—I have to tell the stories I witness.

I assume my first drafts won't be any good—that's why revision was invented.

But that's me—everybody needs to find their own individual path.

Are you a better writer now than you were when you drafted those older stories? You probably are.

Do you understand the world more than you did when you were 12 years old? You probably do.

(I hope you do!)

So why not apply your steadily increasing knowledge and skill to new work?

Try different things. Make every sentence 25 words or longer. Make every sentence five words or less. Do a story entirely in dialogue. Write a story with no dialogue....

My former teacher and friend and colleague, the late novelist Larry Heinemann, always claimed that "revision is where the money is."

Revision is your chance to make sense out of what you've written....

Try writing in the first person. And then just look through the character's eyes and see what they see.

The great crime novel writer Elmore Leonard allegedly said that he always cut anything that "sounded like writing."

You could try that.

Just write the way you talk.

That's one answer to your question.

Another is really boring: treat your writing like a job. Ignore inspiration.

Students ask about "inspiration" all the time and I kind of wish they wouldn't. It's a slippery concept. I think what they often are really asking is—How do I work up enough gumption to sit down and write?

Maybe try this: just do the work of writing and learn to take pleasure in the work itself.

This might sound boring, but it's real.

I know a lot of writers, and I don't recall any of them sitting around talking about inspiration.

But! We can take this in a different direction. Think about what inspires **you.** There must be something, right? If not—**find something**. Then work toward filling your life with whatever the heck that is.

What you're feeling is normal. At some point your true writerly self will emerge.

(Hint: something BIG is always going on).

Everything we do takes time and practice. So be patient with yourself.

2.
You Can Do a Lot with Human Emotions

My very first creative writing teacher was a novelist named Shelby Hearon.

Shelby once told me, "It's never the book in your head." It took me years to realize how true that was!

Yes. That the brilliant idea you have in your head for the story or poem or book, by the time it travels out your fingers through the keyboard and onto the screen, is not the idea that was in your head. It never is.

(But what comes out your head might be better!)

Who are the characters in your story? Are you going for comic or tragic?

The answers to each of these questions will lead to an ultimate answer....

But don't be afraid to change the outline when you get better ideas! It's not a contract!

Once you figure out what might sort of happen, start—writing.

It might help to think of the story as a photograph—a moment caught in time.

The exercises we use in class are straight up writing practice—they're just to get you used to thinking in words and images.

Like with any skill you're practicing (and writing is a skill, not a talent), you will get better at it.

I love it when students relate their writing to the world around them.

What's the world around us like right now? It's sadly messed up, with a lot of material.

Just keep moving forward. (Until it's time to revise).

(Though revision is actually a different kind of forward).

You are going to live a long time—you have time to write all the stories. For today, just choose one.

Write it.

Too much information will kill your story. (Creative writing teachers have a term for this: "the page two info dump" though often the info dump will take place about halfway down page one).

Does the reader need all the background info? Really? Probably not.

People have been trying to figure that out for a long time!

People are individuals and respond individually to what appeals to them. But—time moves on, the culture moves on, and what appeals to people moves on.

The libraries are full of books by excellent writers who are sadly totally forgotten now....

I like to know where I'm heading—on a trip or in a story—but

I have free will and can change my destination at any time.

Still I start with an objective in mind.

I'm not especially witty, but some few people think my writing is funny. I just put people in incongruous and difficult situations and let everything fall apart for them....

I wouldn't worry about it too much...?

Your personal style will develop over time—and change over time, too.

There are a lot of things at stake for all of us, all the time.

Look out the window—we live in an increasingly dystopian society in the midst of a pandemic. What's at stake?

Sure, you can put a dad character in there wherever you want. A good dad, a bad dad, a drunk dad, a sad dad—all these different dads would add depth to your story....

Clichés are popular because they are often true and were maybe at one time satisfying. But you probably don't want to write a cliché.

Try turning a stale idea around. The buzzer-beating shot clanks off the rim....

It might be a very difficult story to write. But give it a try—ambition counts!

For the stories you write in this class, you're limited by a very tight narrative space. So you might want to hold back on all the subplots.

Love your writing! If you don't love your own writing, who will?

Love your writing—but always read it like a writer. Don't be afraid to cut and cut and cut....

(And when I say cut—**I don't mean delete**. Save those words—you might want them later...).

Do you care about your story? If not, please find a way to care about it.

Pretending to care about it will work until you really do come to care.

The real danger is not making any forward progress because you go over and over the same passages trying to get it "perfect."

If your characters cuss, then use real actual no-kidding no-holds-barred cuss words.

I'm thinking romantic love. You can do a lot with human emotions.

3.
Like Everything Else, It Will Come with Practice

THIS IS ONE OF THOSE THINGS IN YOUR WRITING YOU HAVE TO discover for yourself—what works for you, and what doesn't.

And what works for you now might not work later, as your life goes through different stages....

Time works best for me, since I have so little of it.

Some days will be better than other days. There are days when your brain will be dialed-in and the words come almost effortlessly. And—there will be other days....

Characters need to earn the happy ending.

(Of course, what a happy ending consists of is highly subjective. What's "happy" for one reader might come off as "prison" for another!)

Life gets in the way of art, sometimes.

(Actually—*often*).

(Very often).

(Too damn often).

Keep trying different things until you find what's right for you.

Sure, it's disappointing when a writer you like (or liked) says or does something stupid or intolerant or vulgar.

But. I'd still recommend reading good, critical biographies of writers. You might learn something about their process, and you can always safely cancel them if they turn out to be jerks.

Perhaps think of it this way: do you really need a role model? If so, maybe look in the mirror and see yourself as the actual true role model. You know what to do.

The real problem is in life trajectories….

Everyone has to deal with the internal editor. But—the internal editor is almost always wrong!

It's possible to accept that your first draft is terrible and keep moving on, because the real work comes through in revision. So just keep moving forward.

Remember, **ALL TEXTS ARE FLAWED**.

I'm not so sure I have a passion for writing—rather, maybe, I have a passion for understanding the world I live in, and storytelling is how I accomplish the understanding…sort of….

My first memory of thinking about writing was in Fall 1969, reading Tolkien where they're going up into the Misty Mountains and thinking "Wow, I could never write something like this."

(Still true, btw).

Advice to me in the past? Find some way to get over/around shyness, anxiety, and depression.

It's a weasel word, like all other weasel words.

Is it a problem?

I missed four days in June and three days in February. Other than that, I've written every day this year. But I'm in a different place in my life than you are.

You're young—you have time to meander.

It's good to write every day but you shouldn't feel pressure.

(Always good, btw, to keep a writing log. I have a simple excel spreadsheet to keep track of words written per day on various projects).

Long works are always intimidating! Every day I think—omg how will I write 100,000 words!

But you know what? A page a day is a book a year.

Slow and steady really does win the race.

Without burnout.

Telling a story visually and verbally are different things.

I don't know if it's better or worse, but it's something you can do.

I think 1st person/past is easiest, because it sort of kind of maybe mirrors how we (or most people) think.

But 3rd certainly has value. 2nd is mostly writers showing off but can be fun....[1]

Oh, just the usual imagery, language, and genius!

But poems rely on a more intense language....

I don't know how page numbers/story titles/author names can get left off a submission, but they do get left off—a lot. Sad! Writers need to pay attention.

---

[1] This is a joke, in case you're writing 2nd person stories! Really, go be your best 2nd person self!

A voice that sounds like a person talking.

Anything done well is fine by me!

I once answered this question by saying that prose writers think straight ahead, while poets think sideways.

That doesn't help much, does it?

Poetry generally has more emotion in it because there are fewer places to hide. That can be scary!

You should be as specific as possible.

It's just empty words.

You make a statement—then take the statement another step.

This…I do not know.

Read the stories we've looked at so far this semester.

Listen to yourself talk—listen for the punctuation in your words. It's there. Listen for the pauses.

Everyone has a different rhythm. Your characters should probably have different rhythms, too.

It's not that hard. Like everything else it will come with practice.

4.
So Much of What is Considered Success is Luck

Yeah, I'm a huge procrastinator, too.

This works.

You'll have to experiment around and find the best time for you to work. Me, I write at night....

The easiest thing in the world is to *not* write—this is true for everyone

I hate getting started. But once I start, I'm fine.

Most of the time we will never know the actual true honest autobiographical relationship of poet and poem.

I would always prefer that students analyze a text rather than talk about their *feelings* about the text—analysis over autobiography.

A university class is not a book club.

As writers we might well strive to be perceptive, rather than judgmental.

The discomfort perhaps comes as we recognize the limits of our empathy and the difficulty of truly imagining the experience of another human.

Factual aspects of a story can always be researched, and research is always important to a creative writer.

Take your knowledge of these emotions and give them to your characters.

When you're bored with what you're doing.

When you've accomplished one thing and want another challenge.

When your vision of the world changes.

When you learn something new....

All writers have an internal editor. I sure do! As writers we have to find a way to shut up that voice, dodge around it, suppress it.

Keeping notes is a really good idea! Most writers I know have overflowing notebooks with all sorts of ideas and observations....

I think this would all have to depend on the writer and where they are at that moment in their lives....

Said is NOT dead. I would strongly advise you to stick with SAID and ASKED (almost) all the time.

They are meek and inoffensive little words that become appropriately invisible.

When they are invisible, readers can actually focus on your character's brilliant talk.

Maybe try skipping the things you're having trouble with.

Add those things later as part of the revision process...?

Is this truly writer's block or is it truly the voice of your internal editor? Be honest.

Not necessarily.

In a short story, you can get by with only one "round" character. You can distinguish between secondary characters by giving them distinguishing physical characteristics.

(I learned this from my man Tolstoy, in *War & Peace*).

For a long work like a novel, you want to keep character notes just so you don't suddenly change their educational background or eye color or whatever.

You can improvise as much as you like, but please keep notes on your improvisation.

I feel pretty confident starting when I know more or less how I want the book to end, and I have an outline that will get me at least 40 pages or so into the first draft. But even better is a BIG outline.

I use both. I love my little analog notebooks, and I love my phone.

An advantage of the analog notebooks: when you were at a meeting in pre-pandemic times, it was considered impolite to mess with your phone while someone was speaking. But! You could always write in your notebook and say whatever you feel like saying, even if you were slagging the speaker! Try it. It's fun.

Getting any book published is a big deal. After that, you can't control how many people read it, and you *really* can't control who likes it.

So much of what is considered success is luck. But—you have to work hard to put yourself in a position to have luck.

Research! Creative writers do research!

Show their character through action. Just like every day real people show who they are by how they act....

Yes, I think all of us should be writing in response to the pandemic—and everything else going on around us.

This historical crisis we're going through right now is complicated and exhausting—it calls for writers to pay attention to it.

5.
Guilt Won't Get Your Book Written

I THINK AN OCCASIONAL ALL CAPS MIGHT WORK. (SEE JOHN Irving, *A Prayer for Owen Meany*, FOR A GREAT MANY ALL CAPS PASSAGES). Italics are the usual way of emphasizing.

But be careful—readability is very important. And long italicized/ALL CAPS passages are hard to read....

Guilt won't get your book or story or poem written—guilt just makes you feel bad.

Go find something that makes you feel *good*—knitting, fly fishing, basketball, cooking, old movies, video games....

The process of learning something is for me the best part of any activity....

Playlists for books are a great idea. Stories too.

Do it. What music does your protagonist listen to? What do you listen to?

The "real" person will be transformed by the magic of imagination and the exigencies of the story into a brand-new and different "fictional" person.

My response is/was pretty basic—don't base your characters on people who will be hurt.

(Unless you **want** to hurt them).

(Which is always an option).

Your life as you live it is your most precious writing resource. Don't be afraid to use it in your writing.

When your focal character opens their eyes, what do they see? There's your description—maybe, if it's needed.

I actually think Tolkien was doing this....

The best novel? Ever? Oh—*War & Peace,* by Lev Nikolayevich Tolstoy.

You don't want your best writing buried where no one will notice it!

Setting is always important, unless your characters are floating around shapeless in a formless void. Most of the time they are some place.

Remember—the BODY is also a setting....

Probably *The Great Gatsby*, for the punctuation.

Yes—I am motivated by em-dashes and commas!

I may have talked about this before....

You can tag the dialogue through action or setting, too.

What are your characters doing while talking? What are they seeing?

Read your story backwards, aloud.

This removes the context of the paragraph, and you can see

(hear) each sentence in all its glory/ignominy.

Fifty-one years, ha!

You have to be persistent.

I think foreshadowing is best accomplished as an aspect of revision.

In your first draft, going forward, it's more important to just get to the end.

Obvious isn't always bad, and what's obvious to you—the author—isn't necessarily going to be obvious to the reader....

Are they talking on the phone or face to face?

They could be walking, shooting zombies, fishing, watching tv, washing dishes, sitting on the can, shopping, driving, in church, in a meeting, fighting—they could be doing whatever it is people do...while they talk....

Also—it's important to think: are they actually listening to each other?

I mean, really—how many times do people actually fully pay attention to one another?

Good question! I'm trying to figure this out myself!

Try going for empathy.

No one is really *frightened* while reading a horror novel. No one thinks they are actually going to die.

I would keep moving forward and get the story written and then look critically at what you have.

Do you really need a backstory with past relationships? Maybe—but maybe not.

You take something you've written that has a lot of problems (all texts are flawed!) and then you fix the problems.

It takes time and attention and is really rewarding.

I think the aging process has left me more easily distracted than I once was.

The problem with writing is that life gets in the way.

How much time can you afford to spend on writing? For most of us—not enough.

Day jobs are good. Having a roof over your head and food in your belly is probably more important than writing!

A lot of writers do practice writing....

It's great to treat yourself when you accomplish something! Everyone needs to do this!

For me—beer and turkey legs!

6.
Just Keep Going Down One Path or Another

MANY YEARS AGO I WAS A STUDENT IN A CREATIVE WRITING class much like ours and I wrote a story I thought was pretty good. But I know now it was a good *student* story....

What made/makes it a student story? Well, I know for a fact that at the time I wrote it, I didn't know what the heck I was doing....

I did the *right things*, but those right things were a result of lucky accident....

(On the other hand, you could certainly argue that much "art" is "accidental")....

Moral of the story: until you know what you're doing, just be grateful for the lucky accidents!

(Then—once you know how rare lucky accidents can be, be even more grateful!)

There are any number of writers who have gone down the road of pomposity.

The best writers—the best revolutionaries, the best eye doctors, whatever—are all informed by a sense of humor.

My advice—always be aware of life's absurdities and ridiculosities. And embrace them.

My whole life up to the point I finished...?

The difference is—LIFE.

A LOT OF TIME.

Just keep going down one path or another until you find the right path....

DO NOT DELETE ANYTHING! Keep all your variations. Trust me—you have room on your hard drive.

Write a story with a strong beginning.

Oh, inspiration. Well! From looking out the window, from the things I see in life. From dreams. From snippets of people talking that I overhear. From things I learn....

I look at a situation and ask, "What if...."

There are often big big BIG differences between "Truth" and "Fact."

The highly personal voice is always very engaging. You can do a lot with a memoir.

Do you have a citation for that?

(I could also be stupid!)

NO!!!!!!!!!

Borders are interesting—to paraphrase music historian Ed Ward, they are where things come together, and where things come apart....

As noted earlier, life gets in the way. You just have to do the best you can with the time you have....

A novel? One....

Stories? Maybe eight or ten....

People would go crazy for this!

America has always been a tense and violent place.

All kinds of madnesses are out there....

I've had students totally turned off by Christine Granados or Oscar Casares because their characters code-switch English and Spanish. But I look at those writers and see that the dialogue is totally in context and understandable. So—make sure the context works....

I love Tolkien and I would BURN those stupid fucking LOTR movies if I could! Ha!

But—*The Godfather,* Parts 1 & 2, is/are the best adaptation ever. *The Godfather* novel, by Mario Puzo, is very mediocre. But Francis Ford Coppola, in his adaptation, found the inner story and elevated it to greatness. You can buy a book, *The Godfather Notebook,* by Coppola, which contains his annotated copy of the novel and the shooting script. It's a revelatory insight into the creative process....

Oh, yes! Absolutely! You can learn a whole lot about the structure of narrative by watching film. Film structure is different from literary structure in its details, but the scene-to-scene structure can be really helpful....

Each round of revision I focus on something else—dialogue, setting, transitions, colors, textures, whatever....

So: start revising by knowing that your revision will take multiple passes.

Each pass you might focus exclusively on a different aspect:

- character (a pass for each character)
- setting
- scene transitions
- beginning
- ending
- plot holes
- widows & orphans
- weasel words
- Then read it aloud!
- Then read it aloud—backwards!

This is the fun part of writing....

Pre-pandemic I would take a week to 10 days to grade, now with the pandemic friction, it's 10 days to two weeks....

All assignments are good—some are terrific!

I wouldn't worry about plot holes until you begin revising. As you consider (and reconsider, and re-reconsider) your work, the holes will become more and more apparent....

...and you can fix them....

Maybe...try something political and topical? The protagonist's significant other (or father or mother) becomes enveloped in conspiracy theories or fascism or white supremacy. What then to do...?

This is a problem that many, many people are facing right now.

During some of the revision passes, don't look at your story as a whole. As an entire story. As a plot.

Look instead at the writing.

At each sentence, ask—Is this the best sentence I can write?

Seriously interrogate your work and your writerly self.

You'll find things to fix!

Every semester, someone does something truly terrific! You can, too....

Too many students focus on plot. A story is much more than a plot.

Any plot can make for a good story if it's written well.

If you focus on character and setting and language, you'll be successful....

I come up with a character, then find an idea to put them in, then a setting. Then I figure out what will happen (the action/the plot)....

Sometimes that's simple—my current work is a sequel to my last book, so the character and setting are done.

A lot of my stories are set in Austin, so there's a setting I know well. I'm able to visualize my characters doing stuff in the setting....

That's part of the outline. I make an outline and then update it every couple of days—motifs, themes, maps, dreams are all part of it....

Thanksgiving's my favorite holiday! Because I get turkey and beer! Especially now that I'm an adult (an adult for many years) and can organize things however I want and I get *all* the turkey and *all* the beer!

This evening after class I think I'm going to do a zoom happy hour with a friend. And then sleep.

What are you going to do?

Well, stories are about characters. They can have objects, or they can interact with objects.

Oh my gosh yes!

Several students have won awards for work they've done in my classes, and several others have been published.

In fact, two stories from this semester are very close to publishable....

Yes! In fact, you're going to read one of them a couple of weeks from now.

I have a story that was published, and I was still dissatisfied with it after publication. So I revised it while teaching a class of Advanced Fiction Writing, to show students methods of revision....

Towards the end of the semester, you'll read the original version and the revised version, and you are not under any obligation to like either one!

7.
We Are All Complicated!

Sure, it's very satisfying to finish something. Take a couple of days off and be happy, or happyish. Eat a big steak or big tofu or whatever. Take a nap.

But—then you have to get to work to get your project published.

And then you have to start on a new project.

Writing is a way for me to understand the complicated world I have been born into....

Sometimes! But it's changed over the years.

Well, it's capitalism.

Percival Everett once told me that "the writer's true self will always elbow its way onto the page."

For most of us, our fears are very deep and usually unspoken.

We are all complicated!

You can just skip a space, and then the narrator can begin the next section, "Months later...."

The best thing about teaching creative writing in a university is working with energetic young people....

Stories can come from everywhere—and do.

Once a piece gets published, it's pretty much done. But until it's published, feel free to go back and back again, if you want, until you are truly satisfied....

Many writers have a tendency to overwrite the ending. Just cutting off the last couple of paragraphs or so, or even the last words, can be an easy fix to make the story better.

There are few definitive endings in nature, other than death. (Maybe). Abrupt is often better...?

In a short story, you don't want to have very many characters. There's not enough room for them!

I know my first drafts are flawed. I know that every text is flawed. So—of course, I've written a flawed text.

Then I revise—and I fix the flaws.

Or try to.

My advice—accept the flaws and move on and finish. Then fix the flaws.

Of course, I grew up in the 1970s, and these things were little understood....

The more you write, the better you get. It really is a learning process....

Paragraphs!

You probably want to leave with the impression that the life of the protagonist is...going on...but it's going on differently because of what happened in the story....

Answers Without Questions

Yes. Keep moving forward. Finish the story.

Then—abandon it, or revise it. But finish it.

Please don't ever delete your work!!!!!!!! You might want those words later. THEY ARE PRECIOUS.

Well...it took me 45 years to finish writing my first book. But—from first word to final draft? About three years.

The idea what to write—well, I have hundreds of ideas. I'll never write them all. But I try to choose the ones that speak to my heart at whatever time I'd sitting down to begin....

Make significant changes. Look deep into your story and your poems. Elevate them.

It's not enough to merely make minor grammar/spelling/punctuation changes....

For me, the crisis we're living through is a spur to get going and keep going. "I will not be defeated by a stupid bat virus," etc.

Try taking your response to our current situation—anger, sadness, confusion, whatever it is you're feeling—and put it in your writing. Engage with your environment.

"Anger can be power." My boys, the Clash.

Pandemic is putting the kibosh to face-to-face networking.

Keep writing. Keep learning. Support other writers. Be a Literary Citizen.

Make everything better....

There are many ways of telling stories....

8.
Cultivate Humility and Patience

Turkey legs & turkey leg pie!

I've written a Holiday/Christmas story—it's in my book *Burnt House*. It's pretty grim!

I didn't want to drive a cab any more....

People have appetites; how do they sate those appetites?

When people dine together, they talk. Food gives them something to do. (A lot of dialogue I read seems to take place in a vacuum).

Also, food is itself intrinsically interesting for most people. (Always be looking for ways to connect with an audience).

Be humble.

Big picture hope: I'd like to see America healed. If it happens at all, it's going to take some time!

Personal hope: I hope I live long enough to get all my books written. (Which might take a long long time and if I live that long with my brain intact I'm cool with that!)

But there will always be a demand and desire for stories, though there's no telling how they'll be delivered....

I miss hanging around the Teacher's Bar and bragging about my students!

Here's what you need to do—cultivate Humility and Patience.

Writing doesn't happen overnight. Many young writers find this discouraging.

Patience and Humility will win the day.

And I would encourage all of you to follow Lev Nikolayevich's example—be excited about your next project!

I've learned to adapt and survive (so far).

Horror.

Everything is equally easy or difficult, depending on the writer's state of mind....

But here's some advice: don't wait to tell your stories!

I once knew a great story and I sat on it. I waited until I was a "good enough" writer.

And I never wrote it. Still haven't!

I should have written it immediately! It would have sucked, but who would have cared? (Other than my ego). Writing it then would have made me a better writer now.

Moral of the story: don't wait! Write—now.

Everyone needs to read more.

Those of you who already read a lot need to read a lot more.

Those of you who don't read a whole lot need to read a whole lot more.

Every book you read helps build your Writer's Toolbox. You'll have a greater ability to understand all the options you have as a writer.

I think just about everything is important enough to write about—if the writer takes their writing seriously.

And takes the world seriously.

Understanding what a story is, and making it happen....

Go with what's in your heart. That's vague—but true.

What poems do you feel strongest about?

Here's an activity: keep a journal. It doesn't have to be complicated and sound like the all-knowing voice of whatever. Just write down your observations about what you see and experience. It can be a list. Or photos!

(Actually, if you use social media, you are in fact keeping a journal).

The world is always changing and slipping away. Notice the changes! (This takes practice).

Develop HUMILITY and PATIENCE.

It takes a long time to get really good at writing fiction. A writer's ego and perfectionism can get in the way.

And also be PERSISTENT.

Pretend to care.

Make it a game. In the end, everything you write is just words.

Watch how one scene flows into another. Look at how the dialogue is edited and cuts from one character to another. Look for how setting is used. Look for how it is lit and filmed. Read the movie like a writer....

I don't buy it.

Answers Without Questions

That may not be factual, but it's True enough to be a starting point for a novel or a film....

Though I wouldn't want to hang around with him....

The drugs are definitely making him irrational.

Oh, there are pleaseant, easy-going, good-hearted stoners everywhere.

I see him as the innocent victim of capitalism....

Nihilism is the denial of the value of reality, so here the nihilists are the cats-paw of capitalism, which believes in nothing outside of profit/greed/gain....

I liked it. Dark and funny.

We've had some grim readings and viewings this semester—I thought it might be nice to close with a comedy....

The War on Drugs has been a catastrophe for our country.

Food.

This job is easy when you have a lot of great students!

9.
Just Put Down Words One After Another After Another

FAN FICTION CAN BE VERY GOOD PRACTICE.

And of course stories from the Bible, Shakespeare, mythology, fairy tales are all continually rebooted and re-imagined.

Remember—there are only (maybe) three basic stories!

That's a difficult and important question! And—I don't know the answer.

I remember when I was finishing up *Burnt House*—I was totally mentally exhausted, and the semester was beginning and everything was very difficult.

My reading indicates that hating what you do is a big part of burn out, and I really do love what I do.

So—was I just tired?

I guess.

Maybe here's some advice. I haven't worked on my work-in-progress for four days. Just sort of tired of it. And I'm feeling the guilts about being sort of tired of it and slacking off.

But something reminded me of an old abandoned project sitting on my hard drive, and so I opened that up and loved it and worked happily for a couple of hours.

So…maybe try working on a different project to get around burn out?

(If it *is* burn out?)

I didn't write much from 1984 to 1990 or so. I was doing stuff, but not writing. Depressed and angry. But I took a class similar to this and ending up publishing all three of the stories I wrote in it, and I was off….

You can do this, too….

How long to let a project sit? Maybe 20 years? (Sort of serious—look at next week's reading!)

But 20 years is extreme. Sure, let it sit for a while and write something else—maybe a couple of something elses. When you come back to it, you'll be a better, more experienced writer than you were when you wrote it….

Graphic novels are terrific! I couldn't do one—I can't draw and I also don't have enough knowledge to theorize one. But if you have the interest and skill and curiosity—do it.

I like stories that are physical and sensual, not stories that are abstract….

Humor is seems to be totally subjective. A lot of my friends, for example, love writer David Sedaris, and I just don't get him (I love his sister, comic actor Amy Sedaris!) I think America's greatest comic novel is *A Confederacy of Dunces* (it was a big influence on my first novel), and a good friend of mine thinks it's tragic and depressing.

I find a lot of dark humor in Hemingway, and few other people do. And Tolstoy is very funny in places!

Here's a recommendation for a funny writer: Tom Wolfe. His nonfiction book on the space program and the first astronauts, *The Right Stuff,* is a hoot. And his big novel about greed, *Bonfire of the Vanities*, is full of fun unlikable people doing outrageous things.

But what I think is funny you might not....

I think you should share your writing. But not big chunks like whole chapters. Try what Austin Kleon suggests in *Show Your Work*....

Plagiarism shouldn't be a worry. But publishers want first exclusive crack at what you've written, and if half the book is on some lame amateur website they will be discouraged.

Here's an idea: why not start sending your work out to reputable publications? Why not get published for real?

Go for it!

I went to grad school and fell in love with it....

When you think about grad school, look at the professors—look at their websites—find people you want to work with.

And then—also, REALLY, REALLY SERIOUSLY—look at what kinds of financial support they offer....and then compare all the schools and then compare them again.

Do research.

Always do research.

Do writing practice. Maybe try three pages a day (handwritten, in an analog notebook). Do it for a month and you will be a better writer.

What to write about in writing practice? Anything! Everything! Since no one will ever read it, you shouldn't feel pressure from your internal editor.

Just put down words one after another after another.

And read—two or three books a week. Read like a writer—always be looking for how the author did what they are doing....

Do all this and at the end of a year you'll be the smartest person you know.

10.
Experimenting is Part of the Process

Well, I'm pretty much always thinking about my writing (I have writing dreams), so when I finally sit down at the desk I'm sort of almost kind of maybe ready to go....

Almost, because I always have a hard time starting!

I do not write in the mornings.

I don't mean to abuse you if you're a morning person. At all times be your best self!

But my peak efficiency time is from @1100pm to @100am. That's my writing time.

Robert Olen Butler, a very fine writer, in his craft book, *From Where You Dream*, advocates for early morning writing because the writer will be closer to their dream state.

Yeah, Bob—you can sit down and shut up. While you're writing, I'm sleeping....

I'm going to try to write every day this month, but I'm not trying to write a whole book this month....

Try doing timed writing sprints and see how much work you get done....

Hemingway (allegedly) said, "Write drunk, revise sober." But let's assume he was speaking metaphorically!

I try to force myself. Just open the file or the notebook and at least LOOK at the work. And when I look, and I'll usually see something to fiddle with, or more....

No, nothing special for me...

Every writer has to find what works for them....

Experimenting is part of the process, and it's a fun part.

I read a lot of history, and quite a few biographies....

For fiction—recently I've been reading mostly horror and noirish crime....

Sure—travel changes your perspective. It de-familiarizes your base location. You see it new—and this will often emerge in your writing.

And the more observations you make, the richer your writing will/might be....

Discouraged?

Nobody tells me what to read.

Again: it's never the book in your head. It will never be as good as what you envision. Just get used to that and do the best you can.

Also—don't judge your first draft. Really. AT ALL. The first draft only needs to exist for it to be fine.

In the seventh grade I read *The Sun Also Rises*, by Ernest Hemingway. Changed everything!

Some very few people can make a living as writers. Most

writers have day jobs. (Or inherited wealth).

Every character is me, or an aspect of me. Heroes, villains, men, women, dogs, cats, whatever. I always try to see the world through the eyes of my characters....

That said—I'm not an autobiographical writer, I'm an **experiential writer**. I use the experienced observations I make of people and places and things to inform my writing, though my writing is not based directly on my lived events....

Big themes told through the actions and lives of individual characters can make for compelling narrative in either literature or film....

Yes! I think the context is—let's untie ourselves from the past and create a new and free life/society/world....

There's also a line very early in the film—"You live in a place, you should know something about it"—which I think implies that if you truly know something about a place, you can then understand it and deal with it.

Whitewashing the past—or embracing a false past—leads to ongoing problems....

(Like, just take a look around at our vexing current political situations...).

Change is a constant. Young people are always growing up in a New(er) America, where the past is being simultaneously forgotten, rediscovered, and reinterpreted. This can certainly cause misunderstandings and strife!

There is also an inherent conservatism in the way so many people hold onto what they were taught when they were young and how they are resistant to new interpretations of the world....

It sort of seems that corruption is more or less everywhere, and seems to go in waves. Our second Gilded Age—the Right

Now—is sadly extremely corrupt....

Maybe because it's a form of conflict, and most all stories need conflict. And because it's pretty common....

Generations. Borders. History.

The guy who wrote the script for *Chinatown* was inspired by a line he read in an article about the history of Los Angeles: "...at least part of the personality of a city devolves from the crime we perceive to be committed there...."

The crimes will differ from location to location and throughout different eras.

But there is a lot of dark history out there in America, and you don't have to look very hard to find it.

11.
Knowledge is Good!

SOMETIMES I GET ASKED TO WRITE A BOOK OR MUSIC REVIEW. I have a really hard time—the critical hat does not fit well on my ginormous ball head.

Also I have a hard time with academic writing. I usually have to imagine LOVE or HATE for my subject to get going....

I was always reading as a kid. I went with my mom on weekly trips to the library and loaded up on books. And my parents bought me any book I wanted. I started reading adult literature when I was in about the fourth grade or so....

The hardest part of writing might be figuring out what you really want to say. That takes effort and thought but it's part of the process!

Then—you have to figure out the BEST way to say what you want to say, the most expressive language to say what you want to say.

How do you turn up the power of your language...?

Find the volume knob!

(Where's the volume knob?)

One of the most overall useful writing classes I had as an undergraduate was an art history class—we had to write about art! I learned so much!

Try it right now—go find a painting and just describe it. (Trad narrative art might be easier at first).

Then write an ekphrasis....

(I'll wait...).

Other history classes are good, too. (Of course I think this: I was a history major, ha).

Knowledge is good!

We're in the 21st century, so you will also need to know some basic Photoshop and InDesign. These are very valuable skills!

I always wanted to tell stories. When I started college I wanted to be a journalist (I wanted to write A-heds for the *Wall Street Journa*l!).[1]

But I'm too shy and/or crazy to talk on the phone, so journalism didn't work out at all....

Once I set foot in grad school I wanted to be a professor....

But, basically, I'm a boring, linear, word-type guy....

No, not too much. I just move onto something else....

Titles...

When I'm grading or editing, I start by looking at the formatting—formatting errors just jump off the page and into my eyeballs. Sloppy formatting is a bad sign.

If your reader can't easily read what you've written, you have

---

[1] *A-hed:* the oddball feature story tucked away on the front page of the WSJ, between all the economic stuff....

a problem. Think of all those poor confused eyeballs!

Be generous—both with other people and with yourself.

(Writing is an act of generosity).

Perhaps practice writing longer sentences, and embedding your ideas in those sentences…?

Walt Whitman!

I'm not in college anymore, so I don't have to read things I don't like. Or finish everything I start.

It's nice!

In grad school I was reading a lot of memoirs as I researched my dissertation, and I read an awful memoir (I hate it too much to even mention the title to diss it). Dreadful. It was the last book I hated that I finished….

In my downtime from teaching I work on my own books. Also: I drink beer and watch tv….

What a great question! And—there is no definitive answer.

Generally, punctuation is more important in a poem than a story, since there are fewer words in a poem, and every word has to be in the correct context and carry a lot of weight.

But! Sometimes you can remove punctuation from a poem and speed it up!!!!!

Read your poem closely, and experiment. How do you want it to sound?

I go through phases, though I always like reading histories about American stuff in the 19th century….

The ending should be a big part of your outline. Maybe even the starting point!

What I've found a couple of times is that the novel stops

the scene or two before the projected ending in the outline. Just—there is nothing more to say about this story or this character. So: The End.

But the overall tone of the ending itself is dependent on what has transpired in the novel. Triumphant, elegiac, whatever.

And—whatever happens—maybe turn up the volume in writing the ending? (There's that stupid volume knob again). It's the second-most important part of your book.

It's what will stay in your reader's memory.

Also—who gets the last line? This is really important.

I guess some writers do the name symbolism thing. But I'm feeling that character names should just be names.

That said—the name should be appropriate for the characters. Who are they? What year were they born? Where were they born? All these factor into the naming conventions....

Yes...but—

It will vary from poem to poem!

George Martin is kind of an outlier, but at the same time his big novels are still under focal control. (Maybe). (Sort of).

Also—it's a long long series!

(Martin needs to get busy and finish those last two books!)

(Robert Caro needs to finish his LBJ biography, too!)

I would still advise you to limit the number of important characters in your short stories.

Do you really have enough space make them into individuals?

Or will they just be names on a page? What is your available narrative space?

12.
Try Pushing Ahead

OKAY—TITLES. IN YE OLDE FACE-TO-FACE CLASS DAYS, I WOULD often send students out to walk about the halls for 10 minutes and come back with 10 titles. (Everyday objects can make great story titles!)

Or—maybe a song lyric that represents something in your story. Or a line from a poem. Or something odd you overhear while walking around....

We are surrounded by titles.

And—I usually start stories with a title. The title is sort of where I get the seed idea from.

(I have a notebook which is nothing but titles. I'll never get them all written!)

Character names? A really really good resource is the Social Security Administration's baby name database. The most popular baby names, decade by decade.

So—figure out more or less when your character was born, and go from there....

Or—use phone books. (Do phone books still exist?)

For *Burnt House*, I had an ancient West Virginia phonebook and I chose many names from there, mixing them up by first and last names....

Outlining! (Outlines, of course, are my answer to just about every writing problem...).

So I outline, of course. But, yep, I start writing the book or story at the beginning. It's the most important part of your story/novel/memoir/whatever.

I worry most about beginnings and endings...The middle, generally, can take care of itself.

I think it's a pretty good idea to have multiple projects going. You can switch from one to another as your get stuck.

But my experience has been that at some point, one of the projects will catch fire and take over all your time. If that happens, just go with it—you can get back to project B later...

I'm writing a sequel to *Normal School*. It takes place in 2020 and features the pandemic and Trumpism and ghosts.

I haven't generated any new material on it in about six weeks. I'm just too tired. But I have @90000 words written so far, so I work on revisions every day.

And—last weekend I pulled out an old project and worked on it for a couple of days.

There's always something to work on. As busy as I get, there's always 15 or 20 minutes a day for writing....

And 15 or 20 minutes a day is enough.

A page a day is a book a year.

You can republish a story in a book, no problem. In fact, I'd say that's encouraged! Some journals will take previously published work—always check their listings in *Novel & Short Story Writers Market*....

I read a lot of student stories, and I see the huge unwieldy army of characters as a real problem.

When there are too many people in a six-to-eight-page story, there's not enough space for the secondary characters to be even flat characters. They're just names on the page.

And the fact that they stake up valuable narrative space means that the protagonist is given less to do....

Well, both. Sort of. But you need good work for your buddy to promote.

Good writers come out of the slush pile all the time. But you have to put yourself in a position to benefit from any publication.

Hence my encouragement of Literary Citizenship.

Be active on social media, and support other writers. Let people get to know you.

Try pushing ahead. The work that is forced is just as good as the work that flows. Can't tell the difference.

But—you can always skip the tough spots (make sure to update your outline) or bypass a stuck place for something easier.

(Me—I usually force my way through the tough spots).

No—you're fine!

And—a lot of people do this. I'm thinking right now of the Hemingway novel *For Whom the Bell Tolls*. The book opens with the protag laying on pine needles in a forest watching people, and the last scene...there he is again.

(His life has changed a lot in the ensuing few days!)

So—a form of circularity.

You can easily do this in a short story or novel. When you're dreamstorming your outline, just work the circularity into it....

I have a list of seven books I need to write before I die. So—I'm racing the clock.

I'm in my sixties as I write this—will I get them all done? Will my physical and mental health hold out?

We'll see!

13.
Happy Endings Should Be Earned

READING OUT LOUD WORKS FOR ME. YOU CAN FEEL THE RHYTHM of the words tap across your palate....

Well, what do **you** care about?

If you don't care about what you're writing, your lack of care will come through.

That said, "feelings" are usually kind of abstract and hard to write about. Personal experiences are good beginnings for a story, but they need to be better—that is, more story-like—than "real life."

Social topics can work if you don't preach at people—put your character in a situation that illustrates something (like roommate tension during pandemic quarantine, for a very good example).

Like my fave TV series. *The Wire* is the best show in TV history. (It streams on HBO, or whatever it calls itself these days). It's sort of about cops chasing drug dealers, but it's really about people and the problems they have—funny, exciting, suspenseful, heartbreaking—and the society they live in. Covers social topics and doesn't preach.

Most of my poems are short stories that didn't work as short stories—I just keep whittling them down to about 14 lines or so....

And—observations of the world. Something that catches my eye. It doesn't need to be much....

I try very very hard not to get all philosophical....

Don't overthink it. Writing is not (necessarily) about making grand pronouncements on the Meaning of Life. It's maybe more about observing the world and seeing the things that only you can see.

Go look out your window. What do you see? That's your story.

(It may well be that your observations have some grander meaning).

Your observations are enough to start. They're plenty.

Try writing four or five sentences about something concrete you know about. (How to drive a car. How to tie your shoe. How to pour milk on cereal).

Or this. Here's a prompt my late friend Larry Heinemann would use: *Tell me something you know how to do that your parents don't know you know how to do.*

Take about 10 minutes and get back to me.

Elevate your language.

But don't overthink it. Don't try and be profound.

Just look to the world for—inspiration (ha!)—and you'll be fine.

Poems are usually written in sentences—so, just put the commas and periods and em-dashes where they would usually go in any sentence....

(Maybe avoid semi-colons, which I've always seen as elitist punctuation).

(That's just a personal maybe, though).

And, that said—punctuation can be really important in poems. Poems are so short that the punctuation really draws attention to itself.

(Unless, on occasion, you don't use any punctuation at all).

I write about the world I observe or remember...I stay as concrete and real as possible.

You can do that, too!

Just describe it as it is. Later, when you revise, you can search for the right metaphor (and maybe you don't need one!)

Obviousness can be the right thing!

I might add on a technical issue that your secondary characters could become very important as they interact with the protagonist....

Sure! Read a lot. That's part of the research. You want to see what's been done before, so that you can do it better!

That said, happy endings should be earned....

And *that* said—it could and might well be that the problem in the ending lies earlier in the story.

One of my fave writing quotes is by movie writer/director Billy Wilder: "If you have a problem in the third act, that means you have a problem in the first act."

14.
You're Writing about People

KEEP IN MIND THAT YOU'RE ALWAYS WRITING A STORY ABOUT people, not about magic or science. Right? If you're writing fantasy or science fiction, you're writing about people who engage in magic or science. (If your protagonist is a robot, it's essentially a person).

Why is a lot of dialogue a problem? Who told you there's too much dialogue? Not me....

Hemingway was the writer who changed my life, and he was big on dialogue. So, guess what? I've always been big on dialogue! Who's gonna stop me?

That said—if you're a dialogue-heavy writer, your dialogue should be sharp and well-punctuated....

Now I'm scared. Did I not warn everyone not to be literal about "hero sets off" as a story type? Like—it's a protagonist, a focal character. They don't have to be Achilles or Superman or whoever...unless you want them to be Achilles or Superman or whoever....

But, anyway...Me? I don't worry about category when I'm

pondering a story. Character first, then setting, then action. The category will emerge organically from the action as it develops.

(Obviously, I'm not writing for a class where I have a cranky professor who's trying to nudge/push/force me into trying New Things).

I've been reading a lot of detective/crime/noir fiction the past few years. And, as I write this—Elizabeth Hand has a new Cass Neary novel out! And Tana French has a new novel out too! Megan Abbot has a new book coming out next summer! They're all terrific writers—all their books are highly recommended....

That's the function of the outline.

I kind of see the outline as the First Draft. I spend a lot of time on it before I start writing and update it often as I write.

And—outlines for short stories don't have to be detailed—just a handful of bullet points will work. But it's good to have the from-here-to-there thought out, even if you change it as you write....

Most published stories are about 12-20 pages—3000 to 5000 words. The trend is shorter and shorter. There's just not enough space for longer stories.

We go six to eight pages in our class because grading. But—don't stress! Make the story as long as you need it to be....

(That said—if everyone in both classes went three pages over, I'd have an extra 108 pages to read. It adds up).

I'm fond of all my characters. Even the villains.

Tom Holt has been in three books—*Professed*, *Normal School*, and my current work in progress. So I apparently have lots to say about him.

I'm very fond of Linda Smallwood in *That Demon Life*....

I think this might happen more with freelance journalism than with fiction....

But I think it would depend on how you approach it, what kind of limits you set between internal deadlines and external deadlines, and the pressures and stresses of whatever else is going on in your life....

I think about my characters a bit—who they are, how they got to be the way they are. Then play around with an outline. Then I get serious about the outline, etc.....

Great idea!

Novel or story? You probably don't need too many characters in a short story, so introducing new round characters late might be a problem. (A flat character might be easier, since they don't have to be People We Care About).

Adding new characters late in a novel is usually not a problem unless they totally take over the narrative.

(I'm looking at you, Alexander Solzhenitsyn).

If you're with a major press and if the company is making lots of money off of you, they will take care of most of your publicity. If not—especially if you're an unknown writer—PR is up to you. Be on social media, send out review copies, hustle for interviews and bookstore appearances, etc.

Okay, triggering incidents. Where do story ideas come from? Example—my story collection, *The Messes We Make of Our Lives*.

Maybe three of these stories came from dreams—not the whole story, just an image or idea.

(Do you keep a dream diary? You might want to).

Most of the others have a triggering incident that more or less happened in "real life," something that I then applied imagination to and made better than real life.

(Imagination is simple—it's merely looking at something an asking "What if?")

The story "Quiet Sport," for example. I was once fishing the Shoshone River in Wyoming, sort of near a campground just outside Yellowstone. And I was doing my thing, and this kid, maybe 13 or 14, starts throwing rocks right by me! I was PISSED! And I thought—I'd like to throw that goddamn kid in the river. And so I wrote a story where the protagonist throws the goddamn rocking-throwing kid in the river! Ha! Victory! The End.

The story "It May Be a Day..." is also sort of based on something I saw. Back when I was your age, I was witness to a murder. But—when I wrote the story, I wrote it not from my puny witness POV, but from the POV of the murderer. Some months after the murder, a cop told me that the murderer got turned in by his sister. That was my "What if?" moment—I wondered what happened between them. (My first published story...).

And so forth. Moral of this post: make your stories better than real life.

Also a moral—your lived life is your most precious resource.

15.
Your Characters are Hungry

OUTLINES...?

Make a list of 30 things you want to have happen in the novel. Bullet points are fine.

Does your bullet point take up less than 800 words to tell? Well, no it probably doesn't—there is always something more to say about anything.

Don't let your internal editor—the dreaded voice of the adversary—worry you about continuity and/or "quality"— **just keep moving forward**.

Eating is a profound rhetorical connection between writer and reader. So—do it. Use eating.

Your characters are hungry. Feed them!

Also remember that eating is about memory as much as it is about nutrition. (Watch some shows on Food Network and see how chefs and cooks present their food—very often they start with a memory).

Making coffee becomes an anchor for a memory.

Meals eaten with two or more people are about how the people relate to one another.

Go back to Food Network again and see how Guy Fieri describes food. He can be kind of annoying but he's very good at what he does. Watch almost any episode of *The Sopranos*. Read writers to see how they do it. Cook something—eat it. Research is fun!

I always look for new things to try in class—these Participation Questions are a pandemic adaptation....

I would rather not be confused.

People have lives—they are very busy!

Most writers pay—or at least buy dinner for—their beta readers.

This might sound glib, but—can you pretend to be confident?

Most of the people reading your work do not and will not know you. So if you pretend to be confident, they will think you're confident.

Writing is about acting as much as it is about putting words on a screen or a page....

Also, I sense a writer's confidence by how the scenes unfold early in a story. The beginning works, then the next scene takes the story another step, then another. The writer shows that they know what they are doing structurally....

So...maybe pretend to yourself to be confident while you learn various writerly skills...??

For a long time I subscribed to several word-of-the-day email lists, and any word I found interesting would go into my writing. I particularly liked the one with archaic words.

("carking" made it into *That Demon Life*). But imagery can be constructed with basic words, too....

I read *Lord of the Rings* when I was in the 6th grade and I wanted to do what Tolkien was doing. A year later I read Hemingway's *The Sun Also Rises* and it changed everything in my life....

I've had a few poems published, though not many. I tend toward narrative poems—stories that have been stripped down to 14 or so lines....

The writer should always interrogate themselves about how they are using the character who is unlike them. Is the writer appropriating a story? Is the writer stereotyping or exploiting?

The first step should always be empathy. And empathy doesn't come naturally, you have to work for it and learn it.

This is something I do not know! I've had students who write games—I assume there are books written about game-writing how-to and theory....

When I started I was in a class like you all, and I just wrote the story as it came out. I did a LOT of reading outside of the classes—I went to the Best American Story shelf in the library and worked through about 40 years or so, and I subscribed to multiple literary magazines. And I wrote a lot, which is also a way of learning. And as I learned more I became more methodical—planning the story with—yes—outlines, and focusing on revision rather than generation....

I started calling myself a writer fairly late—probably about the time I got the Dobie Paisano Fellowship. Even though I'd been writing for a long time, that was a big external validation....

Keep them simple—only describe what the focal character is seeing/experiencing....

16.
Being Influenced is a Good Thing

WHEN WRITING A FIGHT SCENE, KEEP IN MIND THAT FIGHTING is really difficult. And exhausting. And most fights are settled swiftly....

By looking at the photos, perhaps we become more absorbed into the memory/story...?

I call it a memoir. Or a work of creative non-fiction....

I can get TOTALLY lost in old photos! Sure—I could go on and on.

Women tend to be judged harshly—far harsher than men—for marital infidelities. This is true in fiction or in what passes for "real life."

There are a lot of different thoughts about how to arrange a story collection. I tend to go strongest story first, next-strongest last, weakest in the middle.

A writer writing about a murder in Texas would frame things differently....

Sure—we can look at the photo, read the text, look back at the photo, contemplate the person as someone who once lived....

Guilty.

Yes—I sure do. They really help to bring it to life....

People often feel trapped. Very often. Trapped by economics, faith, gender, family....

So, sure—to a trapped person it might seem easier and quicker to murder your husband than to get a divorce.

Mental health needs to be addressed everywhere!

It's a tawdry illusion with a rotten core...

Memory is a weird construct—it's always changing. Incidents get compressed and expanded and rearranged....

That's an interesting question!

My answer is...maybe?

Family cohesion can help people stay strong in a crisis.

Maybe, sort of...? The Hunter Thompson novel is about the sixties, but it's about drug-induced madness, and not so much about tawdriness and shallowness....

This might make for a good essay question...!!!

The Granados book is set in the right now. But I hadn't considered the time-perspective in the other books....

No, they weren't hypocrites. They were just sinners. They believed and fell short....

It's popular across all of literature. Most stories need conflict—and marital discord is conflict!

Almost all prisoners in state prisons get parole at some point—that's the (theoretical) goal of incarceration—get people ready to reenter society. (Maybe).

In federal prison, you generally serve out your whole sentence.

Murdering someone for the insurance money is not a good thing.

I don't think they have to, but I like it when they do....

I really like, say, Oscar Casares's *Brownsville*. Stories connected by setting.

Sometimes you can get a novel-in-stories, where there is a connecting arc throughout the individual stories. (The kleptomaniac story we read a few weeks ago is the first "chapter" in Jennifer Egan's wonderful novel-in-stories *A Visit from the Goon Squad*).

But even when there is no overt connection, a story collection is still usually connected as a representation of whatever is going on in the writer's head and/or heart at that given time....

Dictionaries and character listings would be a part of the text, and the writer would have control.

Maps? How good an artist is the author? If the map is important and the author is a good artist, they will use the author's map. If the map is important and the author is a terrible artist (like me, say) the publisher will use a map and hire an artist to make it (and find a way to make the author pay for it).

(I love maps—I wish more writers (and writing students) would use them!)

Authors have very little input on covers. Almost none. The books I edit, I discuss ideas with the writers, but the final decision is by me and the press.

For a previously unpublished writer sending something to

a publisher? That ms should be complete. Done. Done and revised until it is as close to perfect as possible. (**Close**—remember, all texts are flawed).

In the meantime, while you are completing and revising, try to get your shorter work published in journals. Maybe start sharing your work online....

For me, one of the marks of a great story is when you shout at a character—"NO! DON'T DO THAT!"

Yep, I sure do show the influence of other writers. Tom Wolfe, especially, bears down on me. But he's sadly dead now and won't have any new books, so I guess I'm safe.

It's actually pretty common.

Some writers I know will only read things way outside their genre while working on a book—pulp detective stories or pulp science fiction. That seems like a lot of extra work, unless you like reading those things.

Better just to smooth it over when you do revision, like spackle.

(I've actually had students tell me that they don't read ANYTHING, for fear that they will be influenced. Please don't tell me this—I will be disappointed in you).

(Being influenced is good thing).

17.
All Your Ideas Have Potential

I WROTE MY FIRST BOOK WHILE WORKING AS A CAB DRIVER (I actually wrote it in the cab, between passengers). Cab driving is a hard way to make a meager living. When I finished the book I thought—Oh! I'll go to grad school and get an MA and maybe a teaching certificate and teach at high school or a community college or a private school or wherever. And then on the first day of grad school I fell in love with it and decided that first week that I needed a PhD.

I'm very lucky.

How does that work? Let's use our imaginations....

Let's say you've written a successful children's book, a fantasy, and you want to write an adult story in the same world. You want to write—oh, a quest story. There's this hobbit that has a magic ring and has to destroy it. The hobbit has to travel a long way—it's going to be a big book! Okay. You make an outline hitting the important action/plot points along the way. And then you start writing. And as you write along, your themes emerge. You find that your story is about—friendship, and honor, and love, and loyalty, and duty. (And about your own unacknowledged colonialist beliefs). And you keep writing. And the plot takes some turns you hadn't expected. (You update your outline). And the friendships go deeper, and the love comes through, and there's a layer of intense aching sadness over everything. And then—after four years of writing—you find what you've actually written is a reflection of your own experience in World War One.

(This is a counter-factual literary speculation—as far as I know, Tolkien didn't use outlines).

(But he should have).

Okay, I'm seeing these as three different things—needs, theme, life lesson.

- **Needs.** Your character's needs are the holes in the character's heart. How is your character damaged? (Just about everyone in this world is damaged). What do they need to be happy? What are they doing to fill that hole? Look back at Monica in "Fight Like a Man"—what is she doing to fill the hole in her heart? You will learn about your character as you write, but you should be at least familiar with them when you start.
- **Theme.** As you know by now, I am a big believer in outlines. But I also kind of think that you should, at the beginning, remain open and uncommitted on the theme of your story. A general idea is good, but you don't need more than that. Let the theme emerge organically from the text.
- **Life lesson.** I would caution you a little about "life lessons." Many readers really really really REALLY resent heavy-handed "teaching" on the part of writers. (I'm one of them). Please just tell me an interesting story.

I guess it depends on what you mean by "success."

But the basic answer is—sure.

Example: My acquaintance XXX XXX is a critically acclaimed novelist and, sadly, their books don't sell enough for them to make a living, so they work a day job for the federal government.

And many, many writers teach.

And, yes—day jobs are a very good thing! Think—**HEALTH INSURANCE**.

The point of the story list we went over a few weeks ago is that any plot/theme can make for a good story—if it's written well.

So perhaps instead of focusing on a good idea, focus on a good character, an interesting setting, and strong beginnings and endings....?

Here are some "plots" from some of my stories:

- woman fed up with her boyfriend
- man returns home to find wife on drugs
- man fired from his job
- woman fired from her job
- there's a fish stuck in the toilet
- man takes drugs, plays softball
- man ignores wife's (very valid) complaints

Kind of boring, right? There is nothing at all exceptional about these "plots." Yet the stories are at least competent because of character and setting and language and they were all published....

All your ideas have potential. You just have to find a way to use language to realize that potential....

18.
It's All Things You Can Learn

WELL, IT'S NOT JUST LIKE YOU CAN WAKE UP AND JUST DECIDE to do traditional publishing—you have to sort of "earn" it. They have to want to publish you. So work toward that. Get your name out there, publish in journals, etc. Do research—

Anyone can publish through Amazon. Which is fine! But are those books any good? Not just as a text—is the book as an **object** any good? Covers are especially hard for beginners/amateurs.

This is why I tell students (here I am telling you)—learn some skills. Learn at least the rudiments of Photoshop and InDesign. Get a website up, and a blog. Use social media. Research book design. Etc.

And then learn some PR—even with trad publishing, you'll have to do much of your own promotion....

There's a lot to this book-writing thing—but it's all things you can learn....

I'd have to see some examples, but—very generally—

A lot of the excessive telling I see comes in backstory info dumps. Solution—get rid of backstory. Most stories don't need it.

A lot of excessive telling comes in flabby third person interior dialogue. Solution—switch to first person, and the narrator can talk directly to the reader.

Very very generally: try staying in the story-present, focusing on action. (Dialogue is an action).

But, like everything else in life—it depends.

Be balanced.

What are your goals as a writer? How much are you willing to work? Will you have to make sacrifices in your personal & professional life?

(I sort of answered this upthread...).

Yes, and I love it. I can disappear down a research tunnel like you wouldn't believe—especially photo archives.

I'm curious—I like knowing things!

Everything I learn has an impact on what I'm writing and on what I've already written. This is one of the purposes of revision....

(One of the purposes of education, too).

I'll repeat here something y'all are probably tired of me repeating—**creative writers do research.**

So, you want to write mysteries? Cool. Start with some research. There is a series called Best American Mystery Stories. Comes out every year. Read the past 10 or so volumes and see what contemporary mystery writers are doing.

While you're reading those mysteries, start going through some newspaper archives and look for obscure, forgotten, and odd crime stories. Small and mid-sized towns are the best. Check and see if your library has a subscription to newspapers.com—it is very helpful (one of those places, as I said upthread, that I can get totally lost in). Think of ways you can make these stories better than real....

And then start thinking about your characters and your setting. Even though plot is more important in mystery than in literary fiction, character and setting are still crucial....

Research research and re-research.....

In the next section of the class we will be focusing on sharing your work....

So—social media, blogs. And then start submitting stories to journals.....

Research...general or specific....

I want to see what other people have done. (How can I improve on what they've done? How will my personal experience make what they've done/what I'm doing different?)....

Then I sit down and start visualizing my outline—and then I write the outline....

I think that just depends on what your personal values are. There's no wrong here—it's just a way of looking at language and looking at a career....

And you will almost surely think differently and write differently as you age....

My advice: get good at something now. You can always try something new later....

If you encounter a wall, go around the wall.

Seriously.

Ideas are very hard to write, which is why I tell students to focus on characters. A character can always do something different and unexpected. They are not hemmed in by a concept.

Your story will succeed or fail based on the quality of the writing, not on the underlying idea or concept....

I'm always looking for new books, poems, stories. That said, I've been using *Ordinary Genius* and *Brownsville* for several years now—they're really good and get across the important writing things I want to get across. The stories and poems in the first part of the semester get rotated around....

19.
Your Heart is Original

I GREW UP IN A FAMILY OF STORYTELLERS. IT JUST SEEMED—natural—to try and take it another step and *write* stories....

The process is pretty basic—you send stuff out, and get rejected, and send it out again and again and again...until you hit a Yes.

Keep moving forward.

It takes only one person to like your work—but it might take some time to find that person. You have to be persistent.

Rite of passage? Sure. Validation is a good thing!

I think it's important to somehow make time to read. Even if it's only fifteen or twenty minutes before you go to sleep....

Most of the time we'll never know the relationship of poet and poem. (Or writer/writing of any kind). Once you get to grad school you'll have theory dealing with the "implied author" but until then just assume that the narrator is the narrator, a character, unless the author tells you differently.

Poems tend to be more personal than stories—there are fewer places to hide in a poem.

Yep. I have lots of journals and notebooks and I use them!

I have a daily planner, a daily diary—both of those are hardcopy—and my Pandemic Diary (on my computer)—I update those every day.

I have an evening diary and a dream diary—both hardcopy—I update those several times a week.

I have several prose notebooks and a poetry notebook—all hardcopy—I update those as needed.

I have a pocket journal I use when I go out in the world, but it's been unused since the pandemic started because I seldom go out in the world....

And I'm on Twitter and Instagram and Facebook, and those count as journals....

Keeping notes is a really good idea! Most poets I know have overflowing notebooks with all sorts of ideas and inspirations....

Prose or poetry, I write to come to a better understanding of the world I live in....it's an absurd and ridiculous and mysterious place! Writing helps me sort it all out....

I can write just about any place that doesn't cause me back pain. Right now—I write in my recliner. I wrote my first novel, *That Demon Life*, in a taxicab...I wrote *Normal School* and *Burnt House* in bed...I wrote most of *Professed* in a coffee shop....

So—I'm flexible.

Except for the back pain part.

Oh, yes—screenplays operate from a totally different

paradigm than prose or poetry. And there are a lot of books on screenwriting.

And—indeed—you can be inspired by movies! I sure am. Go watch *Sunset Blvd* and pay attention to the narrator/ghost....

WRITING IS ABSOLUTELY A SKILL THAT CAN BE TAUGHT AND LEARNED!!!!!!!!!!!!!!!!!!!!!!!!!!!!!!!!!!!!

None.

Because it's not (necessarily) the plot or the theme or the action or the setting that makes a story "original."

It's what's in your heart that makes a story original. It's the way you see the world that makes a story original. It's the way you render the world through language that makes the world original.

That's the whole point of this class. I want you—all of you—to encounter the world through the personal lens of your individual understanding.

Your heart is original. Use it.

20.
Dodge Around the Internal Editor

I DIDN'T WRITE MY FIRST POEM UNTIL I WAS 42 OR SO YEARS old. I was in grad school, and I was working at a really fine literary journal, *Callaloo*.

The editor was a poet, the managing editor was a poet, and the young woman I shared a workstation with was a poet. And so I started writing poems, just to keep up with them all. And I was so lucky, because the managing editor, Adrian Matejka, is a really really terrific poet, and he was around to critique my work. And so I got a few poems published right away....

But! My first poems were all narrative poems. They were short stories that didn't work as short stories, and so I stripped them down layer by layer until there was only 12 or 14 lines left. You can do this too!

I don't know. But a lot, I hope, because you deserve a lot!

(All of you deserve a lot!)

All writers have an internal editor. I sure do! As writers we have to find a way to shut up that voice, dodge around it, avoid it, suppress it.

A trick that works for me: timed writing sessions. Set the timer on your phone for 20 or 25 minutes (no more than 25). Then just—write—until the timer beeps. Do not stop to think! Do not pause at all! Do not take your hands from the keyboard or pen! And when the timer beeps and you're done, go do something else.

This works. I've written several books this way.

You'll have to experiment around and find the best time for you. Me, I write at night, and I'm most productive from 1100pm to 100am.

I'm a huge procrastinator, too. The easiest thing in the world is to not write—this is true for everyone.

I hate getting started. But once I start, I'm fine.

Poems for this class might be best drawn from any sort of concrete (not abstract) human experience—from experience that is physical and involved with the world....

I would always prefer that students analyze a text rather than talk about their feelings about the text—analysis over autobiography. (I'm thinking this is somewhat of a pandemic problem, since if we met three times a week face to face, I'd be bugging people about this constantly). When a person says that they "like" or "don't like" a story, they're not really talking about the story—they're talking about their own feelings.

(Liking or not liking a text is of course fun when you're reading like a civilian, but a university class is not a book club).

The discussion of likeability in female characters is something that has been floating around the literary world for a long time now, maybe forever. We can all see that the patriarchy puts constraints on "acceptable" standards of women's behavior.

Many readers carry those constraints over into their reading, and negatively judge female characters in a story or novel or film. Male characters are usually judged far less harshly than women characters, even when they are doing much the same thing.

As writers we might strive to be perceptive, rather than judgmental. To wildly paraphrase Anton Chekhov, 'I don't need to say that stealing horses is evil. Everyone knows stealing horses is evil. I want to write about why people steal horses.'

(So...why does Monica in the story we just read behave the way she does? (Hint: whatever it is, I'm pretty sure it's not really hypocrisy)).

Roxane Gay has written a terrific essay on this topic. A quote:

> In many ways, likability is a very elaborate lie, a performance, a code of conduct dictating the proper way to be. Characters who don't follow this code become unlikable. Critics who fault a character's unlikability cannot necessarily be faulted. They are merely expressing a wider cultural malaise with all things unpleasant, all things that dare to breach the norm of social acceptability... Why is likability even a question? Why are we so concerned with, whether in fact or fiction, someone is likable? Unlikable is a fluid designation that can be applied to any character who doesn't behave in a way the reader finds palatable.

I get why students push back about certain characters. Most of us resent things that we are required to read. If we're resent-reading a work that has a character who violates our own peculiar moral code, we'll be super-resentful. But.

In short—as a civilian reader, it's (mostly, probably) perfectly okay to find the behavior of a fictional character repellent!

Answers Without Questions

But as a writer—and as a student—you should be analyzing how and why the author created this character the way they are, and how the author used language to get the character across....

It really shouldn't matter whether you "like" them or not....

21.
How a Text Means, Not What a Text Means

Having a super-badass character kind of removes any tension to the action/plot or opportunity for character "growth," if you're interested in that.

They're just...badass. And flat, and uninteresting.

Though maybe the super-badass character is also aspirational for many readers....

Discomfort perhaps arises as we recognize the limits of our empathy and the difficulty of truly imagining the experience of another human. But it can be done! My advice: make your character an individual first, and a social construct second.

Factual aspects of a story can always be researched, and research is always important to a creative writer. You don't just go around making things up. The emotional aspects of a story...that's another job for writerly empathy. We can learn this by watching how people behave in different situations, by imagining how we would behave in a similar situation, by imagining how a person who is not us might behave....

Also: Flannery O'Connor said this: "The fact is that anybody who has survived his childhood has enough information about life to last him the rest of his days. If you can't make something out of a little experience, you probably won't be able to make it out of a lot."

So, think about it: you've emotionally experienced *everything* there is to experience in the world—love, hate, anger, joy, fear, etc.

Take your knowledge of these emotions and give them to your characters.

(Yes, even if your knowledge of these emotions is incomplete!)

Good question!

I would like it if students would "read like a writer." What does it mean to read like a writer?

It means reading for *how* a text means, not *what* a text means.

How the writer used language, sentence by sentence, to construct the story or poem under analysis. How language is used, not necessarily whether it is successful or unsuccessful, likable or unlikable.

It's reading as perception, not judgment.

Look for these things:
- dialogue
- point of view
- tense
- setting
- punctuation
- action
- exposition

Every student in this class can learn about these aspects of fiction from the stories we're reading this semester.

It's maybe like when dreams fade once you wake up. It's

probably important to strike while the iron is hot, before the forgetting mind takes over!

I like much of the Stephen King book, *On Writing,* (I like King in general), but I have a few reservations.

He doesn't seem to understand that his success gives him a level of privilege that less successful writers do not have.

Also, his hatred of academia is grotesque. (Who hurt you, Big Steve?)

But—many students have gotten a lot from that book. Read it and make up your own mind.

(For a similar reason, it's a (generally) good idea to avoid connecting action to dialogue).

Try skipping the things you're having trouble with. Maybe add those things later as part of the revision process...?

Also—is this true writer's block or is it the evil voice of your internal editor?

Not necessarily. The stranger can certainly be the focal character—the protagonist's first day on a new job, the first day at a new school, a traveler stopping to get gas in a new town....

Here's something: go watch these three movies, then get back to me:

- *Yojimbo*
- *A Fistful of Dollars*
- *Last Man Standing*

(Hint: they are all the same story, rebooted over and over again...).

(Also—your focal character doesn't have to be a guy!) (Or a gunslinger/samurai)....

22.
Write for Yourself

So—say you're writing a novel set in New Mexico at the time the atomic bomb is being built. You want to stay pretty close to facts, but you could have your (fictional) characters interacting with real people. Or you could have an alt timeline where everything goes off in a different direction. Or...Or....

But still—and this is true for any *Or*—you'd base your story around research....

Show their character through action. Just like everyday real people show who they are by how they act....

But—you don't have to write about the big picture, and maybe probably shouldn't. Focus on the personal and the small.

Don't make it the last six months—make it 15 minutes out of the last six months....

A student last semester wrote a FANTASTIC story about pandemic roommate conflict....

It can be done!

That's what fiction does best—focus on how people live their lives.

Please don't distract your reader.

I like them.

They demonstrate something about writing that students need to know.

I do.

But—really, not necessarily autobiographical. Just something you see/hear/touch transformed into a—story.

Go read some writers from @ 120 or so years ago—someone walks into a room and there's page after page of room description.

Yeah. No. We don't see the world like that anymore.

Your protagonist walks into a room. What do they see? What do they see that's *important*?

Focus on what's important.

Shoot me an email saying that you want to meet up, and we can decide on a time that suits both of us....

Then—we get on zoom—

It's always good to see other people when you talk to them, and see the occasional cat or dog wandering around the room....

Where? There's no "One World" literature....

What is success, anyway? As far as the US goes...*Gatsby* was out of print when Scott Fitzgerald died. *Moby-Dick* was forgotten when Herman Melville died. They both died thinking they were failures.

Me, History can look after itself. I try to live in the near-future and recent past....

Some cases of Writer's Block are a form of depression and can be treated with SSRIs. Most (way the most) cases of writer's block are merely the voice of the writer's internal editor telling the writer that they are not good enough. We all have that voice. The trick is—to slip past it and get work done....

We can discuss "how-to" as the semester progresses.

You don't. At all.

Once a story (book, poem, whatever) leaves your hands it's not yours anymore. It belongs to whomever reads it.

And—they might not like it. You have no control over this.

What you have control over—total control over—is the text itself when you create it.

Write for yourself.

23.
What You are Writing is Good Enough

Nope, no prescribed topic.

The creative writing teacher and novelist John Gardner once said that there are only three basic stories:

- the romance or relationship story
- stranger rides into town
- hero sets off to find their fortune

So…if he's correct, no matter what you write, you'll end up writing one of those stories. You'll be fine!

(Is Gardner correct?)

Nope. In fact, I wish more students would write horror.

Me, I'd just read the whole thing. It's short….

There are indeed reasons for this—very good reasons, to my mind

Thanks for asking this question!

Yes—our class is a little literary community. And we Venn Diagram out into the larger Literary Community….

You sure can! Start a conversation! Express yourself—

That's a good thing!

But if you have a problem with being on camera, that's fine. Put yourself first.

(Last semester a young man zoomed in from a hot tub. He won the semester).

Sure—every text has multiple audiences. Here are some that you will have:
- Me
- The other people in this class
- An ideal audience that you would like to write for

Keep all of them in mind. At the same time, write something that reflects your own heart.

It's tricky!

In our zoom meetings, I'll go over these questions and answer some of them at length, and maybe I'll go over a story or two or we'll look at some slides or whatever, and just talk about writing....

Basically, we'll sit around and talk about writing. That's my teaching method....

It might be nice to read it before class, but not required....

I sure hope so! But people are individuals and will react individually to different things.

Maybe an appreciation for the complexity of this beautiful and fascinating and tragic world...?

Nope. We will press on relentlessly.

The pandemic teaches us to be flexible and resilient. If we have to cancel a class meeting...we'll find a way to change the schedule and get around it....

But usually—almost always—setting....

Where we live affects how we live. A story set in the gloomy rainy forests of the Northwest will have a different feel from a story set in the arid sunny Southwest...And the characters will be doing different things and have different priorities....

Just do the work.

I often get this question in my creative writing classes. My usual response is, "You don't have to 'like' something to learn from it."

(That said—it's more fun when you "like" something. Maybe you should try pretending to "like" something).

You can also make the class into a game, to keep yourself amused. (This is how I got through grad school).

One of the cool things about teaching a class is that I get to choose books/movies I like....

But as the course proceeds you will see, I think, that there are thematic connections between all the works we look at....

That makes a big difference in how we relate to one another.

We are going to cover the books faster than I would like (or you would like, probably)....

But the readings slack up toward the end of the semester....

There are a lot of places that have used copies of these books—so, shop around.

As I think I said upthread, I think you will see themes emerge. The texts talk to one another....

I deal a lot with writer's block—both as a novelist and as a teacher. Most of the time it is merely a writer's Internal Editor telling the writer that what they are writing is not good enough.

Answers Without Questions

I am here to tell you that what you are writing—what you *will* write in this class—is good enough.

The trick is to find a way to believe that and integrate it into your writing/studying practice....

24.
Rehabilitate Your Darlings!

My fave form of visual art—painting, probably. Though photography is great, too.

In class I just run some slides past you....

It's pretty basic—environment, violence, race, family, gender. How do these elements work in the texts we cover...?

So, sure—

Books that speak to me. Books that speak to the diversity of the Southwest. Those are the main criteria....

Grading is the least favorite part of teaching!

It's WORK!

What makes grading difficult is knowing that so many students place such a weirdly high priority on their grades....

Basically, go north on I-35 until you hit Wichita, Kansas. Then hang a left and keep going west until you hit the Pacific Ocean. Everything to your West and South (your left) is the... Southwest...of the US....

At one time Tennessee was the Southwest. (Ohio was the Northwest!)

But you can see how this concept was formed, right? By someone standing in Boston or New York and looking—West....

But think. How did the people who lived here in the "Southwest" conceive of where they were...? (Yes, there were people living here...).

Write a (good) short story.

And you definitely want to pay close attention to the Christine Granados book....

This is a tough question! Every writer we read will have an individual style....

Don't be a perfectionist.

Nothing is more deadly to a writer than perfectionism.

Know that whatever you write will be flawed because ALL TEXTS ARE FLAWED.

Accept that, and work to making your text better.

And, most of all: KEEP—MOVING—FORWARD

There's a Tolkien line: "Love not too well the work of thy hands and the devices of thy heart...."

That's less violent than "Kill your darlings."

Me—I send my darlings off to the gulag for re-education and rehabilitation. They might be useful later.

Rehabilitate your darlings!

The books are all available at the library. You can also find cheap used copies.

Believe it or not, the books I've written are all faves in different ways—they all speak to different aspects of my personality and writerly being....

"Write what you know" is an old-school convention that privileges experience.

Still, it's not totally wrong! (Or wholly right).

There are a great many different ways of knowing. (Physical, emotional, etc).

You can also write what you learn. Creative writers do research!

Probably the best way to get a feel for short stories is to read short stories. They are actually very odd constructions.

Observe the world. That's it!

Pay attention to the world around you.

Imagination is very simple—it's just looking at something and asking, "What if...?"

So—see things and then apply imagination--

You rely on your memory and your observations of other people.

You've been sad, right? So remember what that was like and paste that emotional memory into your character.

This is sort of what actors do! This is how writing is like acting—you are inhabiting a character.

Please do!

Too many students sadly end up taking a very bland approach to their writing and end up writing about...nothing....

Funny odd bizarre openings. (Please see the story "Chango" by Oscar Casares).

Oh, writing a good short story is much much much harder than writing a good novel!

Short stories have to be really super focused. Novels can spread around all over the place....

I'm very happy when students are deeply engaged in the real world and write about all the problems that arise from the real world.

I got some great pandemic stories last semester! I'd really like to see MORE!

Try writing longer sentences—70, 80, 100 words....

I don't actually forbid writing about serial killers in my classes—I just say it is really hard to do. If a student is up to the challenge, then go for it. I admire ambition.

But sure—why not write about murder? In the past five years, I've received 59 stories that had murders in them....

Life. The world I see around me. I write to understand the world.

25.
Don't Give Up So Easily

I'LL ASK YOU A QUESTION. DO PEOPLE LIVE THEIR LIVES OR SEE the world differently right now than people did in, say, 1900? See—as in "experience"?

(You weren't around in 1900, but you can guess....)

The class is "creative writing," and I have long felt that CW classes don't spend enough time on the actual creative aspects.

Criticism...as in people hated it?

Depression and grief. These are deeply interior emotions/ states of mind that are difficult to write.

How to display them? Here's one way: have a secondary or tertiary character interact with the depressed/grieving protagonist and get them out of the house and make them— do something. Demonstrate the interiority through action.

Anger is also, interestingly, apparently difficult for some people to write. Very often written depictions of anger turn out as sarcasm or snark.

All of these emotions are difficult to write, maybe, because our society disapproves of their open display...?

I just sort of visualize what happens in the story, then I make a quick outline—bullet points for the title and character names and the basic action. Then—I write. I assume the beginning will be bad, but I know I can make it better with revision.

For many stories, it's best to start as close to the ending as possible. Go ahead—try that.

I guess I still have a soft spot for the novels of James Michener, who had huge bestsellers in my youth and is much forgotten today (except for his charitable contributions, which last on in his name). I liked a few of the techno-thrillers of Tom Clancy before he got too right-wing political.

I like Stephen King a lot, though by now he's such a part of our popular literary culture that he transcends high/middle/low culture formulations. The crime novels of Elmore Leonard are in a similar cultural position.

He's my advice: don't feel guilty about any work you take "pleasure" in—music, film, books, food, whatever.

Pleasure is very often hard to come by in this world. Take it when you can.

But we can go over them if you want!

Transitions between scenes are important. When revising, take a pass focusing just on transitions.

For the how-do part of your question, look to our readings. They all do this really well, especially Jennifer Egan's "Found Objects."

Please be careful with some writing software! Students in the past have had trouble producing properly formatted stories (and, yes, formatting is something I notice!)

But you should always know the tools you use.

I was mainly talking about length and complexity. But movies of any kind differ from prose stories in that they are totally external—they're visual, and basically unable (even with a voice-over) of getting into a character's thoughts.

Or you can get really close inside the character's head. Don't write the story—live it through the character's awareness....

I've been writing in first person a lot recently. I am interested in voices, and how we communicate. (Or, very often, don't communicate).

I often push some students toward first person also—it's easiest....

Background in a short story can be dangerous. It's easy to get carried away!

Try to stay in the story present as much as possible....

A short story outline need only be a few bullet points—a title, character names, a few bits of action that will happen in the story.

Novel outlines are more elaborate. The outline for my work-in-progress is at 24 pages and will be longer....

I've known so many really good young writers who just—quit.

I always wonder why people give up so easily.

(Please don't give up so easily).

There is always peer pressure to like certain artists. You can always focus on their craft, if not their content....

But you don't have to like anybody you don't like.

Try using a world that's already created—like the beautiful and mysterious world we are lucky to live in.

Also—try writing about action—about people doing things. Not about abstractions.

Too many metaphors and similes can get in the way of the narrative.

An engaging character (usually). The threat doesn't have to be overwhelming....

26.
You Will Fix the Flaws in Revision

SHE WAS INTERESTED IN OBSERVING NATURE AND THE WORLD around her. Simple as that.

Well, just about everyone who doesn't live in a crystal dome or a cave has to deal with weather. But the weather is different in different places.

I think the ending is perfect.

Wealth and power almost always do win out, sadly!

But I really do think that where we live affects how we live, and so geography is important....

They sure will!

I'd advise you to just read everything....

And read closely. You'll be fine....

They probably have the same effect. But it's interesting that artists build off of one another and are influenced by one another. No one works in a vacuum.

Our old friend J. Frank Dobie wrote a couple of books about lost treasure—but he was presenting it more as folklore than as fact....

I had a great uncle who moved out to the Mojave Desert when he retired. He got water trucked in—once a week a big tanker would come and fill up his cistern.

So—if I had water delivered, sure, I'd be fine living in the desert. Otherwise I'd be reduced to dust....

It might come up. Aridity always lurks in the background in the Southwest....

Here is a hint: when I'm writing an academic essay, I assemble my quotes first. Then I write the text around them. This way I am always on topic and never have to waste time hunting for a quote.

Every book has its points!

Keep alert for these things and notice how they are used and what they mean in the context of the readings and you'll be fine....

Sure. What do you need to know?

They will be about concepts, and how they relate to the readings....

Do the readings and think about how the texts talk to each other. What are they saying?

Hmmm. Let me ponder on that....

I like the dreaminess of the prose....

You could be like Dave in "Ah, Love...." and just brush your hair and jump into the story. Or maybe spend some time visualizing it, and then ease in....

Starting stories is difficult for all writers. I know it is for me! I usually visualize, then make my outline, then try writing the opening....

It's important to know that whatever you write will be flawed. Know the flaws—love your story anyway.

You will fix the flaws in revision!

I would wait for asking for help (with exceptions) until I had something—a page or two—a good idea of where you want to go....

(I'm the exception—you can/should always ask me whenever you feel like asking something!)

Twelve lines, fourteen lines, something like that. Not too long.

You can start anytime you want! Your writing time is—yours—

Set a timer. I do this.

I set the timer on my phone for 20 minutes and I write. I write and I do not stop. I don't stop to check email, I do not stop to think. I put words on the page for 20 minutes.

And then I'm done. And I go do something else.

I can usually get 300 words or so. Do that every day and that's enough for a book a year.

BUT....

If you think you have writers block you should examine the apparent source of your block. For most people, the source is the voice of the internal editor telling you that whatever you write will be worthless. It is the voice of perfectionism. It is the voice of the adversary. You have to find a way to silence that voice.

For me, silencing comes when I accept the fact that my early drafts will be flawed and knowing that I can always fix the flaws later.

Take this one idea away from class: ALL TEXTS ARE FLAWED.

See the answer above. The timer really helps.

I totally suffer from this. I'll do anything to avoid starting, which is a form of anxiety. But—once I find a way to start, and the timer is running down, I'm fine.

27.
Make Your Characters Half-Crazy and Wholly Odd

I GET IDEAS FROM THE WORLD AROUND ME.

The world is filled with all sorts of odd people doing all sorts of weird crazy things.

You know thousands of really good stories. We all do!

Because...it's all drafts until it gets published....

You will always be working to make it better....

Make your submissions DOUBLE-SPACED, please!

I will have trouble reading it if you don't!

In this particular case I think it might be a good practice to make the story revolve around something you know about or have experienced or have learned through research, while at the same time make the focal character someone who is not like you.

I don't know if there's any real downside to it. Except maybe you'll eventually run out of things to write about....

Sure. Look at the stories we've been reading the past couple of days—there are no cell phones! Which is an indication that the story takes place in the past.

Most of the stories we've read for this class take place in the story "past" and use time as a setting. "Indian Camp" takes place about 25 years before Hemingway wrote it. "Pugilist at Rest," about 25 years before Jones wrote it. "The Difference…" about ten years. "River…" is more or less contemporary….

So—if you use time as a setting, you have to consider how people of that time lived and behaved—what were they eating, what were they listening to, how they spoke. To get this right, you have to do research! It's not that hard, really. You just have to be curious.

I give you a list of things to look for. Then you just get in your groups and talk it over….

Maybe try writing long, winding sentences—150 words or so—have the imagery shift abruptly….

Make them dreamlike, not essay-like….

Focusing on action instead of character. Focusing on action instead of language.

The list we looked at last week proves that any action can work…if it's written correctly.

So——perhaps focus on your overall story, and not on the action

Can you do both?

It would be great if y'all formed a little community of writers. It would also be great if you used the awesome resources of the university writing center!

Make an outline.

How long is your story going to be? Six pages? Five? Eight?

Okay—outline.

- Page 1: opening
- Page 2: something happens
- Page 3: something happens
- Page 4: something happens
- Page 5: ending

Here's how that more-or-less works in "Indian Camp"

- They go across the lake
- They deliver the baby
- They find the dead husband
- They go back across the lake

Boom! You have a concise on-target story....

Sadly, a lot of students deliberately choose to write boring stories. True! Many student writers are afraid that they will be judged by any odd weird unethical actions of their characters, and so write characters that are bland bland bland.

Further, many other students mistakenly think "realism" is boring, because they think their own "real life" is boring and in their attempts to write a "realistic" story, they deliberately make their stories...boring.

Sad. When I look around the so-called "real world," I see a place that is full of nuts and oddballs!

How to avoid a boring story? People it with interesting and odd people! There are a (practically) infinite number of human behaviors! Just pay attention to the news—look at all the absurd ridiculous weird things people do!

Make your characters half-crazy and wholly odd, and your story will never be boring!

28.
There is Always a Way to Write Something You Want to Write

MAYBE ESTABLISH THE THREAT EARLY IN THE STORY, IN THE first couple of paragraphs or so. Make sure the reader knows the threat. Make the protagonist totally oblivious to the threat while they go about their lives until maybe page three....

This where your outline comes in. You make a list of what you want to happen in the story—not more than four or three things—and you stick to those actions. That's enough.

The reading load in (English) grad school is very heavy, and I know many people who lost their ability to read for pleasure, since they were reading analytically so much. Sad! That luckily never happened to me. I treated grad school like a job, and I did my job and then I watched TV and read for fun.

But also—for me, reading like a writer and reading for fun are very similar activities. I'm always looking for how it is done. How did this writer use words to get the story across? Why did that writer use so little dialogue? Etc. I find it fascinating, and I learn from it....

So, advice: as you read, keep in mind that the text you're

reading is a deliberate creation of a human, composed of thousands and thousands of individual decisions. Why did the writer make those decisions? Are they decisions you can emulate? Are they decisions you should emulate?

When I write a short story, the title almost always comes first, and is itself a metaphor (or an "inspiration," ha!) for what happens in the story. For novels, the title will usually/often change over the process of writing, as my conception of the novel will change....

I too faced this situation when I was an undergraduate. I remember staring at the textbooks for Theories of Mass Communication or Economics and my eyes glazing over and my brain melting....

If you're like I was, you lose motivation, probably, because you really don't *want* to do the assignments your professor assigns you.

(You do have free will, however, and can always refuse to read things you don't want to read).

(Warning: this will probably negatively affect your grade).

(I tried this as an undergraduate. Don't be like me!)

How I got around these inclinations in grad school: As I said upthread, I treated it like a job, but I also made a game out of it. I would *hate-read* a text, disagreeing with everything the author said. Or—I would *love-read* a text, enthusiastically and rapturously adoring everything the author said.

And, in every assignment, I would look for and find something that I was interested in. There is always something! The world is an interesting place.

If you're busy (we're all busy!), it might be best to make a time. My own peak productivity happens between 1100pm and 100am, so that's when I write. Your peak productivity will no doubt be at a different time. Find it and focus on it....

It might be difficult—but not impossible. Develop your empathy. Do research.

(Yes, I'll say it again: creative writers do research).

Easier would be to have the protagonist, who has not been to war, encounter and know a veteran. Or a family member of the veteran who experiences the war second-hand....

There is always a way to write something. You just have to think it through....

It...depends. If you're writing a fantasy set in some similar medieval-Europe world, then we already sort of know what that is like, and you can slowly introduce the magic. Similarly in a SF story on a spaceship—we know what that is already. You can ease in the science or whatever.

Writing about a totally different world? You'll have to do more explaining—and this can be done well (see N. K. Jemison's *Broken Earth* trilogy) if you put some thought into it....

29.
Surprise is a Very Low Level of Discourse

I haven't really used synchronicity as a story device per se, but I have noticed it in a story or two. But the use of any device will be different for each individual reader and writer....

As always, your outline is important.

Here's something: I know writers who draw little boxes, one box for each page, and list what happens on that page....

Oh, gosh....

(Four sentences—sorry!)

Hmm. Yes....

Combining research and inventive imagination can be challenging but it is essential....

I would advise you to lay off on the army of characters. There is not really enough space in a six-page short story to have a bunch of people milling around philosophizing. They just become—names. Very difficult to write this.

Try to keep to one central focal character, the protagonist....

I'm sorry—I don't know how to answer this question. I'd have to know what the conditions are before I could comment...??

If you want to meet with me immediately after zoom class, we can go over it, and maybe I can be of use....

No! Your protagonist should be as real as you!

"Likable" in student stories too often means bland and boring. Real people can be likable or unlikable, but they are always weird and unique and interesting.

To paraphrase writer Roxane Gay, We don't read to make friends.

I look out the window. Our world is magic. It's weird and it's full of crazy interesting people.

I get questions like this occasionally, and I'm never sure what students mean when they ask about genre—so I'll ask you: What do you mean by genre?

To me, genre is simply fiction or poetry or creative nonfiction. But...I kind of think you're talking about something else.

Over on the Facebook group for creative writing teachers a few weeks ago, this topic came up. Other professors were getting this question and they were baffled, too. Someone explained that what's probably meant is the categories of books as they're listed in a bookstore—urban fantasy, gothic romance, steampunk, young adult, whatever. In other words—marketing.

Is that what you mean? If you want to define your writing by these marketing/branding definitions—that's fine!

But I don't look for this kind of "genre" in your writing. What I look for when I read your writing is—the quality of your writing. I want to see writing that comes from your heart.

Sure, you can go over-length a little bit.

I'd have to look at your story to see what you mean, but—setting should be in every sentence, in that it influences everything that happens in a story. (Where we live affects how we live). You (usually) don't need big chunks of description.

So—I guess keep the action...?

I love them all, for different reasons.

Right now, I think about that dead monkey head because of its weirdness....

(And I'm kind of wishing more student stories were—weird).

No—please do not do this. Novels and short stories are very different in this respect. Stories need to be tight and focused and built around the psychology of an individual. Please make the story as tight and focused as you can.

It's absolutely natural!

Many times, I get to the end of something I'm writing and go—"I didn't know I knew that!"

(And I'm a writer who uses outlines. But! I update my outline every day).

"It's never the book in your head," said my first (and best) CW teacher.

I start at the beginning. And—that's usually the part of the story that changes least through revision. The beginning will (usually) contain the trigger that gets the action moving. It's where I begin visualizing....

I could see where visualizing how you want your character to end up might work, too....

Develop a sense of empathy.

And do research.

Also question yourself—ask yourself why you want to write this story right now, at this point in your life....

Here's a way to do comedy: you put people in absurd situations and play it straight. Don't make it a joke!

Make the characters absolutely serious about their absurd situation. That's funny!

How a story is told is just as interesting—maybe more interesting!—than what a story means or what happens in a story. Surprise is a very low level of discourse.

30.
Everything Gets Better With Practice

Sure—use an email as part of a story.

This is how I do it: Move the margins in, use a different font. Include From/to/subject....

In my novel, *Professed,* I used emails and texts instead of chapter breaks....

I've collaborated with another writer—on a novel, not a story. My partner would sit and write a stream-of-consciousness few pages, and I'd go through and find a sentence or three or five and build a scene around those sentences...It worked pretty well!

But—you have to trust your partner, and you have to figure out how best to work with one another.

Each partnership will work differently....

I put all my thoughts about the novel in my outline....

- lots of quotes from other books that express ideas that I am reaching for....
- some themes that I want to get across

- more quotes
- a list of character names (and how they die/leave)
- a list of things to remember about characters (eye color, etc)
- list of what happens, chapter-by-chapter and scene-by-scene (in this example, 142 chapters/92 scenes)
- a list of plot holes
- when I filled the first list of plot holes, I made another list of plot holes
- some extra things I need to add
- revision schedule
- research/reading rist
- favorite lines from the book

It depends on the story—but, sure, there can be too much dialogue in a story. (There can be too much anything). Talking is just one action that a person can do. What other actions can your character perform that exhibit their personality...?

You just have to go by your heart and by your experience as a reader—these two approaches twine around one another....

Something I've learned: most students write too long and go past where the story actually ends....

(Look at Percival Everett's "Afraid of the Dark"—the story ends perfectly when there is nothing left to say....).

Character is at the heart of story, so I know who my focal character (protagonist) is from the beginning. Then I think a little about whether to go 1st or 3rd.

In a short story, it's important to maintain a consistent POV. Remember, you're (usually) focusing the story through the eyes of a single person.

Everything gets better with practice.

If you self-publish, you're going to have to do it all on your own—the interior book design, the cover design, the story editing, the copy editing. That's a lot! If you want to do that, you're going to need to learn InDesign and Photoshop, and you'll need to study the elements of good design.

It can be done, though! Perfectly legit!

Seeking an agent is a long process—and you will start by research. Recommended: *Guide to Literary Agents*

My novel outlines, however, are pretty darn detailed....

I usually read through your practice writings. But I envision these writings as your space to do your writing practice...so, in a way, it might be kind of intrusive for me to be commenting too much....

I think this is just the typical sexism of the last few centuries—if you read older writers, you'll see nature referred to as a woman, nations referred to as women, states referred to as women—mountains, ships, the sea...a way of phrasing that maybe we're moving beyond.

Though—just last week I heard a politician on TV refer to Missouri as a she ("...she is one of our greatest states....") and ships I guess are still shes.

Past tense works best for me, but you and every other writer is going to have to decide on that for yourself. I've never been able to use present tense satisfactorily—even though a couple of my fave novels are written in present. My brain doesn't work that way. If yours does—good!

Just write what happens without the "suddenly."

Example—if someone starts choking at the dinner table, just have them start choking and keel over. You don't need to announce it with a—suddenly!

31.
Lower Your Standards

I HAVE THREE SOLUTIONS TO THIS APPARENT PROBLEM—ONE mental solution and two practical solutions.

1. **Mental Solution**—get over whatever sense of perfectionism you might have.

    In other words, lower your standards.

    Just write something! If you finish it, it will be fine!

    A draft only has to exist. Nothing else.

    Please remember this: ALL TEXTS ARE FLAWED.

    Your text, my text, the texts of Hemingway, Morrison, Oates—all flawed.

    ALL. FLAWED.

    Instead of perfectionism, try to develop a sense of curiosity about your work. Think something like, "Gee, I wonder how this story will turn out...."

    Remember: It's never the book in your head! And it's never the story in your head, either. And—know what?—what you end up with will probably better than what's in your head. You'll never know until you sit down and write it.

2. **Practical Solution One**—Please never ever delete your words! They are precious. You have room on your hard drive. Save them. (Though my friend Jamey Hatley recently made an interesting post on the need to sometimes let words go...).

3. **Practical Solution Two**—Stop writing on a computer. Use an old-fashioned analog notebook. You can't (easily) delete sentences or paragraphs! You have to keep moving forward! And then when you finish your flawed draft, you'll type it in to the computer, and that will be the first level of revision.

Don't ever delete! Keep moving forward!

For fiction, I've been reading horror or noir (or horror/noir) and then rereading some faves. Nonfiction—history, politics, science....

I'm usually reading two or three books at a time....

Intense language is concrete and physical. Abstract language is...vague. And abstract.

Emotions by themselves are abstract—they are feelings that exist inside your body. You then use language to convey the intensity of the feelings.

Hard concrete sensual physical language.

I agonize a lot—getting started is very difficult for me. But finally I quell the anxiety and get moving and I'm fine....

It's about the same, I guess. Doesn't take as much time.

The main difference is that there's no place to hide in a poem. The "real me" has characters and settings to hide behind in a story, but in a poem the "me" is out there, even when writing through a persona....

Raising the intensity of the language. School has taught most of us to write as blandly as possible, yet the vastness of language is there for us to use. It takes time to figure it all out.

Some people do that! Hunter Thompson allegedly retyped *The Great Gatsby* all the way through to better understand how Fitzgerald's language works. Re-(re-re-re-re-re-)-reading something probably has the same effect. (I've probably read *Gatsby* at least 50 times).

My favorite character? Probably Linda Smallwood from *That Demon Life*....

A page a day is a book a year.

Most writers have day jobs. Day jobs are important! Writers need a roof over their heads and health insurance and turkey legs in their bellies and beer!

Once again: a page a day is a book a year.

If you're dedicated, you can carve out 20 minutes a day to work on your book. And that's enough!

Start at the ending? (Seriously).

Many students avoid conflict in their writing because they are nice people and don't want conflict in their lives.

Yet most stories need conflict. It's pretty simple:
- Person A wants X.
- Something Y gets in the way.

(Y can be a person, a snowstorm, a dog, a heart attack, whatever).

But the conflict is based on the want of Person A. Person A's desire.

What do your characters want? (If your answer is "happiness," please rethink your answer).

The escalation of conflict will depend on what the character wants.

(Notice that I said upthread: *most* stories need conflict. There are story paradigms that do not rely on conflict.)

Also, truly, what I said upthread: A page a day is a book a year.

32.
Just Be Kind

WORK ON YOUR BOOK 20 MINUTES A DAY AND YOU'LL BE FINE. Now—you'll be reading and thinking and pondering outside that 20 minutes, of course. But that's the fun part!

I sort of answered this upthread. But I will expand a little....

Remember: the great Shelby Hearon told me that it's never the book in your head. THIS IS TRUE. The book (story/poem/screenplay/whatever) that's in your head is ideal and perfect. It's golden!

The book you write will be flawed. (All texts are flawed).

If you focus on that golden dreamy ideal you will be disappointed in yourself. You will hate your work.

I DO NOT HATE MY WORK. I love my work!

I have low standards. I know my book is flawed. I trust myself to fix most of the flaws.

I focus on reality.

I pretty much think a child POV is the hardest to write. We're adults, and we more or less think like adults. Children think like—children. It's different, and difficult. Also there is a sad tendency to sentimentalize children and childhood. It's hard to get around. A really good example of doing it right would be "A Long Day in November," by Ernest J. Gaines....

Give it time. (Hard to do in a 15-week semester, I know!)

Let it set. Think about it from different angles.

You'll figure it out....

Great question.

When reading someone else's work say some positive things (there is always something positive) and point out some problems (there are always some problems).

Say, "That ending really works!"

And ask, "Is that paragraph too long? You might want to break it up...."

Just...be kind. (Pointing out problems, btw, is a kind thing to do...).

Many young writers are fragile. (I sure was!)

So here's a place to use the good 'ol Golden Rule—critique others like you would like to be critiqued....

Start.

End.

Try rereading the stories we've had this semester. They all have different endings, and are all excellent.

I would caution against striving for originality at the cost of your overall writing. Just be—functional. It's perfectly okay to have an ending that just sort of...stops....

Think about starting a story as close to the end as possible.

This concentrates the action and reduces unnecessary backstory....

Nope, a nice paragraph is plenty....

...they'd have to be really good words...?

I'd like to see you writing in sentences....

But—always—run one by me and let me see what you're trying for....

It's actually mostly the same—words and sentences....

Freedom to do—what, exactly?

As I said in the syllabus—if you write something racist or misogynistic, I will call you out.

Boom! It looks good.

Here you go....

Theme very often emerges through serious revision. A story might mean one thing while you are writing it, but upon reflection and rewriting, you will see things in the story you didn't know you knew before....

So—at this point I wouldn't worry about theme too much....

Choose the story that's closest to your heart. It's that simple—and that complicated.

We will be talking about revision the last two weeks of the semester....

Try to make the whole story hang together like a snowball....

I saw an interview he did (with Oprah, I think) where he said punctuation is a barrier between readers and the meaning of the words (serious paraphrase there).

Yes! There will be some less-violent, less traumatic readings starting next week!

Yes to all of the above—but, beyond that, consider Evil....

Oh, yes. People around the world consider America in general to be crazy violent, and Texas/the southwest in particular to very extremely massively crazy violent....

Such a great question! And a complicated one! Some writers are better at violence—they see the world as a dark place and go there in their writing. Other writers are willing to go to the violent place but lack the inner darkness to make the violence real.

And, yes—some writers are indeed scarred and traumatized by their own imaginations/writings....

Maybe a better question might be—What does the violence *mean*...?

33.
Your True Self

Percival Everett once told me that the writer's True Self will always elbow its way onto the page.

Yes. And the connecting thread between all the different things you write will be your personality. Your individuality. Your True Self.

I'm not sure I understand what you mean by...style...??

I really like Kim Addonizio's poetry exercise where one object is in love with another object! It's clever and fun. Building/writing a personality into something inanimate is surprisingly difficult....

Write in longer sentences....

You can always come to me!

Strong word choices for sure.

Writing is not a talent. Writing is a skill. It's something that is learned.

Some people learn at different rates. Some people started at different times. Some people are going to be filled with love and desire and curiosity and will persevere. Some people will get frustrated and quit. Life will get in the way of many people.

People are, in short, individuals. And the future is unwritten.

As for writerly success—or, "success"—that is an artificial construct that is mostly (if not wholly) based on luck. Though of course you have to work hard and be ready when the lucky opportunity comes your way....

Wait until you know what you have. I mean, you haven't written your second story yet. And probably haven't revised anything yet....

So...wait....

Sure. But funny for adults might be more interesting than funny for children...?

Oh, heck no!

Shoot me an email and let me know what's wrong. Or we can meet on zoom....

Try not to look at it like you're writing a poem and there's all this incredible pressure to come up with something poem-y....

Maybe instead look at it like a little tiny story. It has a narrator. Something—the trigger—caused the narrator to pay attention. What does the narrator have to say about this triggering incident?

Paycheck and health insurance. As simple and as bourgeoise as that!

I sadly usually just push through. I wish I had a special technique to offer!

I get "inspired" (ha!) by what I see in the world, by what I remember. Though I'm not so sure I'm driven by inspiration. Or "inspiration." I think I write to better understand this complicated and confusing world....

I read *Eugene Onegin* about 50 years ago. Memories are dim. (But I have vivid memories of Pushkin's story "The Shot," which I really loved at the time). I'm not so sure that translated verse from the early 19th century is going to be that helpful to most young writers—but if it is to you, that's great!

I think poets who move to prose are often striking in the beauty of their language. They pay such close attention to every word!

Jim Harrison is one....Patti Smith, mentioned above, is another. And Mary Karr. My poet friend Honorée Jeffers has a new novel just out, and it's terrific....

As for you, perhaps focus on the shape and structures of fiction. How do your scenes work...?

Nope. You'd have to pluck out my eyes and erase my memories first....

As long as the poems we've been reading. How long are they? Use them for models....

They are both writing about the creative process, though coming at it from different directions....

You mean—looking like the writer is relying too much on a thesaurus?

Try writing angry, try writing happy, try writing in love, try writing in hate....

The vivid emotions will (perhaps) lead to vivid language.

(You don't feel these emotions? Pretend to feel them! Writing is often very similar to acting!)

Three lines or more? A block quote....

Less than three lines? Work it into the paragraph....

War crimes are not okay. Neither is torture.

(Do I really need to say that? Sadly, I do).

Yeah, that's right. Perfectionism will wreck your writing.

You need to realize that ALL texts are flawed, and that anything you write will be flawed. And always remember that you are smart enough to fix (most of) the flaws.

A draft only has to be complete. That's its only purpose. Suppress the Internal Editor long enough to finish a draft and then...fix it....

34.
Don't Be Safe

HERE'S AN IDEA: MAYBE DON'T WRITE YOUR FIRST DRAFT ON A computer. The temptation to delete sentences and paragraphs is too great! Write your draft in an old-school notebook. You can't delete anything. You have to keep moving forward....

He is contrasting the intimacy of the inside with the immensity of the outside....

But—also yes, I do think that the texts we're reading speak to one another....

Some of the themes might be the same, or similar....

I'm not sure gore per se is the problem. It's the darkness of the gore—the nihilism behind the gore. How do you capture that on film?

And how do you translate McCarthy's prose into something visual?

I'm sure it could be done—but it seems to pose difficulties—

Life gets in the way of writing, especially this year....

I think the ending of *Blood Meridian* makes it seem...even worse. Something more grotesque than anything that has happened yet...Something indescribable....

Even the witnesses are at a loss:

> Good God almighty

> What is it? He didn't answer. He stepped past the other and went back up the walk. The other man stood looking after him. Then he opened the door and looked in.

My grad school steps to writing an essay:

1. I come up with my thesis first. What do I want to argue?
2. Then I find quotes from the texts....
3. Then I sit down at my desk and I
    - Write my name
    - Insert page numbers
    - Write the works cited

(These three things are important and I don't want to forget them!)

4. Then I insert my quotes....
5. Then I write the essay around the quotes...and, usually, I do timed writings of 20-minute sprints, followed by breaks....

This may not be the most efficient paper-writing method, but it got me (a terrible student) through grad school.

And/But: every writer needs to find their own method....

The pandemic teaches that we must always be prepared for sudden changes....

More lighthearted, more relationship-based, though not always with a happy ending....

(Just about anything is more lighthearted than *Blood Meridian*!)

(Historical accuracy was not a priority in Hollywood movies of the time (maybe is still not!))

Be funny and quirky! Even better—be yourself!

Contemporary poets you should read: Honoree Jeffers, Roger Reeves (an Aggie!), Jericho Brown, Natasha Trethewey, Yusef Koumenyakaa.....

Yes. I want you to BE BOLD. Don't be safe—don't be afraid. BE BOLD.

Take chances.

(Seriously, if you can't take chances in a class like this, when in life will you take a chance?)

I try to write a paragraph or two about something interesting. Then I play with line breaks....

Don't philosophize. Avoid abstractions.

Do they tell a story? Is there a progression? Or should they be random?

Well, it's Las Cruces, New Mexico. More or less.

Sometimes you have to change things around when writing a book. And when you change a place too much—it's no longer the place you started writing about....

Example: *The Kings of Infinite Space*, a terrific novel by James Hynes. It's set in the capital of Texas—Lamar, Texas. What? Lamar? I asked him about that once, and he said that to accommodate the plot, he had to change some of the geography of Austin. And when you change it past a certain point—it's no longer Austin....

35.
It's Better Just to Fix the Flaws

YOU SHOULD START DURING THE LAST COUPLE WEEKS OF CLASS, when we will be discussing revision....

Sure. But you should love your work, even if it's flawed.

It's better just to fix the flaws. And easier.

The better poems and stories have feelings behind them. Do the writers themselves have feelings? No telling. They might have feelings—or they might be pretending to have feelings.

But the poems and stories themselves are imbued with feeling.

The title might be considered the first line of the poem. It alerts the reader to what is coming....

You need titles (see answer above). Titles are easy—the world is full of titles.

Comedic is good. Comedic with soul is better.

In this class? Sure—that's what our Writer's Practice exercises are for—to give you a chance to start poems and stories....

Sure. Time is an aspect of setting. And I usually argue that setting is more important than "plot." So if you're writing historical fiction, you should probably stay accurate to the historical period. If you're not, you're writing fantasy...?

By the way, if the pandemic is not in the stories you're writing this semester, you're writing stories that take place in the Before Times. In other words—you're writing historical fiction. Plan accordingly.

They will be connected by—you. They will represent your view of the world....

Yes.

Sure. I mean—how would I know if something you write is fictional or not fictional?

A good way to write a poem or a story is to pretend to be someone else! Write in that person's voice....

Maybe think of....

- Illusion versus Reality
- The Past versus The Present
- Memory
- The different ways families interact
- The American Dream

Because that's how people speak....

Sadly, some people are totally turned off from anything not personally "relatable" to themselves....

Americans in general are, and always have been, pretty violent....

My favorite book is whatever book I'm working on at the moment right now today! True.

And that's always the case, I think.

If you're using Word, please please please remove the extra

spaces between paragraphs. Those weird spaces make your work difficult for me to read....

Make sure your name is on it!

Darker is pretty much always more interesting and relatable.

You could write light-hearted comedic dark!

Brenda Ueland said something like writing teachers should never "talk about their own work, except to disparage it."

Yeah, no. I think it's kind of important to talk honestly about the process of writing.

Brenda Ueland also said, "The only way to become a better writer is to become a better person"—and that might be true, so I guess I need to work on that....

Soon.

(It's taking longer than I'd like, too).

Yes...

- (legible) sans serif font
- double space
- name
- page numbers
- if you're using Word, remove the spaces between paragraphs

(I don't know what color-coding means...?)

But. I don't know—my worst stories are probably some I wrote back in the 80s that are luckily lost, I guess.

I give a lot of thought toward the characters, since characters are by far the most important element of a story....

Well, yes, I would be wary of exclamation points!

But you can show excitement—happiness, anger, whatever—

with strong language, especially strong verbs.

And your sentences—how long are they?

Here's a couple of paragraphs about music:

> Okay, and this is what people were waiting for—the noise, the Nihilists. Some people leaned forward in astonishment and delight while others leaned back in revulsion and delight... A couple of other people got up and jittered around, too, not really dancing because the music—the noise—was too fast and weird and nonrhythmic to dance to, all they could do was jump and flail and spazz around and totter.
>
> And it was all just really, really *loud*.

and

> So. Lonnie Hudspeth and Vic Reid, Austin cops, were taking a break that night at the Jack-in-the-Box next door to Raul's, eating burgers and curly fries, when some rackety loud *bom-bom-bom-boom* started coming from the bar, booming banging through the wall.
>
> Reid was slouched over, half asleep. But now he sat up. He said, "Damn, that shit's gonna knock a filling out."
>
> *Bom-boom. Boom-boom-bom. Bom.*
>
> There wasn't even a rhythm. Just booms. Thuds. Boms.
>
> Noise.

36.
Political is Good

Introducing...as getting their names out...?

It gets boring to have, over and over, "Hi! My name is Jonathan!"

Instead maybe have...

> Jonathan came into the room, looking tired.
> He said, "You wouldn't believe what just happened!"

Not necessarily. That's the default setting on Word, so you see it a lot. But it's up to you....

You're a smarter, more skilled writer now than you were even a couple of weeks ago.

So—revise away!

The emotion and originality will still be there, but you will showcase it better with your increased skills.

Create several scenes.

Answers Without Questions

Your story is (usually, often) built around your character wanting something. So, a scene. A door opens and someone comes through it.

Who is the person? What do they want? Write it and find out. Maybe whoever it is wants something other than what your character wants....

I want you to write something that
- comes from your heart
- is important
- speaks to how we live in America

Dialogue is a good thing. If it's done right, you won't have too much of it (even if you have a lot).

Look to the stories we've read, and will read. The dialogue in all of them is excellent.

What are you seeing when you read it? Notice where the punctuation goes. Notice where the tags go.

Just do what the other writers are doing.

Well, if you're aware of overusing certain words, you can always rewrite the sentences to get rid of said overused words.

It's an important issue! We will discuss this at length during the revision section of the class....

Try it!

For formatting? Indeed.

If you want to use the same characters, that's fine. But a continuation...? I think that would devalue the first story, and maybe the second....

Sure. But poetic doesn't mean using the fancy-pants three-dollar words from your thesaurus.

It means seeing things in a personal unique way. It means

putting some emotion behind your sentences.

First person or third? First person is easier. You can do more with third, but (too) many times the narrative is very distant and sounds like an essay....

Students often play it too safe. Are too bland. Are afraid to write about anything with strong emotion.

Suggestion: BE BOLD.

Ominous and unfinished is good! The most common problem I see is an ending stretching out a paragraph or two too long.

Political is good! I wish more students were political!

But—you're not writing an essay about politics. You're writing a story about people who live a political world.

(We *all* live in a political world).

Write about what's in your heart....

It's a beautiful book....

Huge! The culture is strong and important, and the stories are compelling....

That's a great observation! The format does suggest frazzled, separated lives....

It's taking longer than I'd like....

One—sure. Of course.

The focus is becoming somewhat more personal. And—that was intentional....

I don't think you need to translate—the context is usually pretty clear.

Sure! I like doing that....

She's interested in her hometown (her previous book is set there, too), and she's interested in the lives of women and their positions in family and larger societies....

People, probably. Or, more precisely, people living in their environments!

Soon...?

Stories about people and their lives—yes.

I read everything twice. It takes a while. Or longer.

Reality vs Unreality is a big one....

"The American Dream" is another....

What do you feel strongly about? What's in your heart?

37.
Don't Make the Reader Do the Writer's Work

I'M THINKING THAT CHARACTER IS PRETTY MUCH THE MOST important aspect of a short story. Think of a short story as a photograph of the psychology of an individual at a discreet moment in time. Without a character—the individual—you have nothing. Action is the least important, probably.

Maybe.

Not enough of a sample size to see any real trends. I'll go over the list in class....

Sure...? What do you want to know...?

When people are interrupting one another, the em-dash is your friend....

I have not—it's on my list!

I don't forbid writing about serial killers—I try to strongly discourage it. The problem is that (most) students who write characters like this aren't willing to explore the psychological depths of the characters—the weirdness, the violence, the evil. Also, the writers don't do enough research.

Want a good serial-killer novel? *Zombie*, by Joyce Carol Oates. It's horrifying and chilling.

My fave horror? I guess *It*, by Stephen King. He's able to connect the cosmic horror to the everyday horror.

I think there's so much potential for conflict at jobs. At workplaces. Just about everyone's had a crappy job, and not enough people write about it....

You're not alone. We live in a stressful time. The students you see around you in their little zoom boxes are hurting. The faculty members in their zoom boxes are hurting, too.

Be kind to yourself. Be patient.

Be kind and patient with yourself—and with all the other little zoom boxes you encounter.

I'm not sure what you mean by motif...?

Believability. There are an almost infinite number of ways for a human to behave—so you can have your character do almost anything!

But! You have to use language to make that behavior truly believable.

Well, I'm writing one—so, of course!

The pandemic is maybe the biggest historical event of the last 80 years. There will be fiction set in it....

Didn't you say you did a lot of writing on your phone? If you're stuck on your phone....

- Try writing on a tablet.
- Try writing on notecards.
- Try drawing a map of where your story takes place
- Try drawing panel cartoons of your story
- Try visualizing your story.

- Move to another room and write.
- Go sit in your car and write.
- Drive around, look at stuff. Ask "What if...."

I do use it every semester! The stories are good, and if you want to learn how to control POVs, you won't find better examples....

In creative non-fiction, you're taking fiction techniques and applying them to something that actually happened. The *actually happened* can be personal—a memoir—or something researched....

Anything you can personalize will be stronger. So—don't be afraid to take your experiences and then fictionalize them—make them better than real life!

Conflict is...pretty simple. One person wants something; someone else (or something else) wants another thing.

You can give a bigger overview of the situation. You can play with irony.

Stories are a bit too short for that, I think. It would be kind of confusing.

Try *Fight Like a Man*, by Christine Granados. It's terrific!

The writing.

I'm pretty sure that people don't change—they just gain some experience and react to their environments in different ways. But their innermost secret self remains the same.

Here's something that will work: put your character in a situation of extreme stress. Arrested, or fired from a job, or in a car wreck, or something. Anything. Then see what happens to them in the next 15 or 20 minutes....

Upthread I said I drive around and look at stuff. I do, and I see stories everywhere. We are surrounded by stories....

If you're overwhelmed with all the stories that are possible to write—just be random. Flip a coin or whatever....

The ultimate success of your story will depend on the writing, not on the concept or action or "plot."

They are all equal. What separates one story from another is the execution.

And—I don't get inspired. I just set my timer and write.....

You're writing about a person, not all people. An individual. So a name is needed. A character is needed.

Endings can be ambiguous (see many of the stories we've read this semester), but there has to be an ending.

Don't make the reader do the writer's work.

38.
No More Cheesy Than You Want it to Be

HOW DO PEOPLE BEHAVE WHEN THEY ARE ANXIOUS? I'VE SEEN people shut down, and I've seen people get agitated and talkative. People are individuals. They react like individuals.

Write about your character doing something, and in doing that something they will exhibit their anxious behaviors....

Find a good title.

Look for titles in—the world.

The title is like an umbrella that covers and protects your story...it can also be a GPS that gives your story direction.

The title is a guide that will point the way to the ending....

It's more difficult now but people still move back and forth for jobs and shopping, etc. And trade between the two nations is immense.

It's creative non-fiction. It's a memoir told in an episodic narrative....

Pilar says, "Everything that went before, all that stuff, that history—the hell with it, right?"

Sam agrees with her. They're going to (try to) live their lives despite history....

It absolutely did! And he sees that he had misjudged his dad his whole life.

Not getting along with parents is pretty common. Family conflict is a real thing....

The different POVs are just different ways of approaching a story. Some more personal, some less personal....

Maybe because fiction can tell a story better than memory, which is spotty at best....?

But it is essentially her own story—she's just added to it, and rearranged it, and created composite characters....

I think real places make everything in a story—fiction or nonfiction—so much better....

No, there isn't much of a plot! But is there much plot to life itself? She's trying to give a portrait of what it was like to be alive in this time and this place....

There are just a lot of different ways to tell stories....

Well, you want to make your stories realer than real. The mere fact of applying language to a life story is going to shake things up and move things around....

No—she thinks her past is important. That her life—and the lives of her family and community—had and have meaning. She's just trying to share that meaning....

Wherever you go, you drag the past along with you.

Take more time. Don't look for an overall "plot." It's just stories about her family....

Oh my gosh yes. People in power want to control all narratives, especially narratives of history. This is going on all around us right—now.

Well, the book is True. It might not be wholly Factual....

It's built off of the photos—they are the base for the stories....

"The Pandemic teaches us patience...."

The language, the images, the reflective comments on the photos....

Ha! When I say "begin a story" it's just an acknowledgment that you don't have enough time or space to write a full complete done finished story during a seven-minute writing exercise....

Fall. Just because it's the best time of year....

Whatever I write will be flawed. I will fix it later.

So—quantity.

Get to THE END—and then make it beautiful.

I'm not a writer who ever feels really "inspired." I just do it....

That said—it's good to think about why so many writers consider writing to be so hard.

Do painters complain about the difficulty of the canvas?

Do guitar players complain about how difficult it is to get started?

Why do young writers talk about inspiration? Why is writing so difficult?

(*Is* writing so difficult?)

Anything can be too cheesy. But romance stories are/can be great.

Answers Without Questions

Look around—there are pair-bonded people all over the place. Each of those relationships has a story.

Stories with bonded people can be job stories—bank robbers or terrorists or schoolteachers, or they can be road trip stories. Or new kid stories. Or adultery stories. But each one will be about the dynamic of one person and another person. (Or more people). (Or people and things).

Nothing is any more cheesy than you want it to be.

39.
WRITE BANNED BOOKS!

I'LL REMIND YOU AGAIN: A LOT OF AMERICAN HISTORY IS pretty darn grim. It's important to acknowledge that and understand that....

Yet there is a trend out there in our great land of rednecks trying to ban books from public libraries. Resist this.

You're writers. You have a stake in literary freedom.

Read banned books.

WRITE BANNED BOOKS!

Sometimes. But in recent years, I listen to mostly instrumental music while writing—lyrics distract me. That didn't use to be the case and is no doubt an aspect of aging.

Do you make playlists for your stories? Some writers do!

Suggestion: make music playlists for this class and for each story....

Writing energizes. It's like teaching—I always feel good....

However! That's only the immediate feeling. I've noticed that if I write, say, say, every day for a month, I'll be mentally exhausted by about day 28 or so. A friend who is a poet reports the same phenomenon.

SO—maybe it energizes and exhausts!?!?

What does it do to you?

Here's an activity: try making a word count of each scene in a story. Then take the data and make a pie chart. (Below is a chart I made of Percival Everett's "Afraid of the Dark"). Look at all the scenes you've written. Why are some scenes big? Why are some scenes small? Which are important? Which are inconsequential?

Revise accordingly.

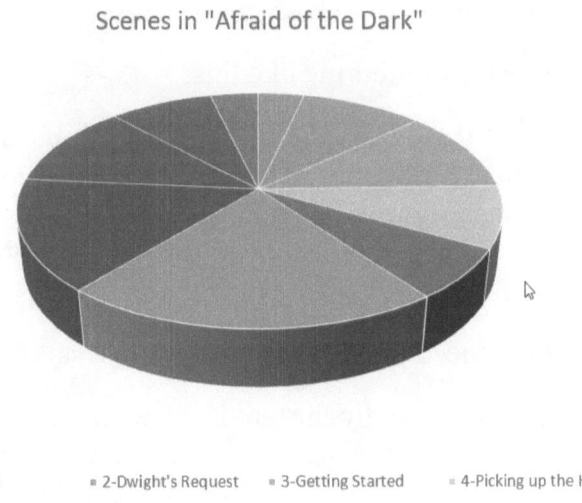

To show elapsed time, just skip a few spaces, and then say something like....

"Six months later, I walked into Darcy's room—alone....."

Or whatever...the time has elapsed....

Oh, in an old-fashioned old school notebook! I have far more control over the composition process. Big advantage: I can't delete anything. I have to keep moving forward until I finish. Also, I can take it anywhere and write anywhere....

I'm at my peak between 1100pm and 100am....

In my chair or at my desk, depending on what stage of the book I'm in....

Rain is nice. (Rain is always nice).

But everybody's different. What about you...?

I'm not sure I know what you mean by genre...??

Do you mean topic/subject matter/theme? We get a lot of stories about students. Which makes sense....

You might write something like this:

> I looked at the desktop and I saw that it was cluttered with withered yellowing manuscripts, twisted computer cables, empty bottles of hand sanitizer, and a sad lone old tube of chapstick. I looked over at Danvers and I asked, "How do you get any work done here?"

But you don't need to write it that way. Just say....

> The desktop was sadly cluttered with withered yellowing manuscripts, twisted cables, empty bottles of hand sanitizer, and a sad lone old tube of chapstick. I asked, "How do you get any work done here?"

Or you can just go through the ms and rewrite any sentence that uses the word "I." Just use search and replace to find the offending words...then fix them.

Also consider—how much is too much? Some narrators might be really totally focused on themselves and use "I" more than other narrators. Something to consider!

Funny and helpful!

Nope! Please try to use "said" and "ask" only. It doesn't get repetitive! Because those are simple, boring words, they "disappear" and all the attention will be focused on what your characters actually say....

"Indian Camp," maybe.

(I just watched the PBS Hemingway documentary. It's worth your time).

Maybe more than three? After that, they're just names.

There are exceptions to every writing proclamation, but you need to think about the wildly constrained narrative space of a six-page story. There's just not enough room for a lot of characters.

The author in that book is attempting to use Literary Theory to find out the Truth of what happened.

(Spoiler: the Truth is not found).

40.
Choose by What's in Your Heart

Sure, you can have action associated with the dialogue. Sort of like this....

> "Well, maybe," Constance said. She pursed her lips like she was uncomfortable. Silent. She turned onto Juniper Street, the campus ahead with its grim ugly dull red brick buildings. The parking lot. She finally said, "I don't know what to think."

But try not to connect the dialogue and the action. Like, don't do this:

> "Well, maybe," Constance said, pursing her lips like she was uncomfortable....

When it's all connected like that I just think it weakens the actual words that are being spoken. It's distracting.

You can fight me on that, if you want.

Getting a box of my newest book for the first time is always nice. But—winning the Dobie Paisano Fellowship saved me and made me. A big deal in my life.

Just mentioning the song is good. But you can also talk about how it makes your focal character feel....

I'm not sure about questions, actually. Let me ponder that a little....

I think you should choose by what's in your heart.

The portfolio is to demonstrate what you've learned in this class—but remember, it's also a representative of who you are as a writer and a person....

Well, they won't be anything more than names. So—that might work either way. But without names, all the attention will be on the named characters....

Either. Or Both. Go read Joseph Heller's *Catch 22* and see how it's done....

You could absolutely do that! A great idea!

Formatting will be important, so that we can understand what's going on....

Maybe add zoom or facetime so there will be some visuals...?

I want to read this!

Write for 10 minutes. Deliberately write the worst writing you can write. This will confuse your perfectionism, since you can only succeed by being terrible....

(I'm serious. This is an exercise I've done in face-to-face classes a few times).

Don't be afraid to make the reader uncomfortable. But if you're not willing to do that...go ahead write about something comfortable....

I think it's a cultural thing....

That's difficult to answer! What do you think?

And, as I've said before, I still have great affection for Hunter Thompson because I loved him so much as a teenager. Though I'm no longer a teenager and can see his faults.

I don't really "take points off" when I grade. I look for things that are good—and I *add* points....

But—I'll do it. I'm in my sixties (today's my birthday!), so retirement is getting closer and closer....

Guilty.

Ideally, your experiences in life give you some perspective and depth in your outlook....??

Interesting. I guess...a place that people have ruined...?

Though complicated!

I'm guessing they were thinking of living happily ever after....?

I would hope that you come to appreciate where you live. Wherever you live, I'd like you to look at the place and reflect on all the stories that have taken place there, throughout history.

The world is a palimpsest.

Where we live affects how we live....

You nailed it! I've thought for years that the best part of workshop is not getting feedback about your stories, but *giving* feedback—learning how to read critically, and being exposed to more stories....

I have a couple of friends that are beta readers and I always look forward to what they say. And I usually hire a copy editor to look for typos and miscellaneous grammar/spelling/punctuation problems....

Sure. You can revise all the heart out of a story and leave nothing but a bland block of words.

Just about everybody improves over the semester. Don't know if it has anything to do with me—it's mostly people applying themselves....

Sure! Of course! It always comes back to what's in your heart.

41.
Some People are Going to Hate Your Writing

I'M NOT MUCH FOR OCEANS OR BEACHES OR SUNSHINE. I LOVE the mountains, and I love hardwood forests like you get back east. Also—just wide open spaces where there's nothing—eastern Montana, for example, or west Texas, or Chase County Kansas.

Fly fishing was a big part of my life for many many years. I drifted away from it when in grad school—just not enough time. I should take it up again. I still have fly fishing dreams several nights a week....

Grading is unpleasant no matter what. It's work.

I find stories more interesting, but poems go quicker....

Sometimes a long time—years. But usually a few weeks, a time in which I'll be working on a different project. Then when I'm ready to revise I can look at it freshly and clearly...

That's easy for me—I've never been able to make present tense work to my satisfaction. So I write in past tense.

That's not all writers, though! Just me.

My advice—experiment. Maybe start your story in present. Then try starting it over again in past. Which is best—which feels best?

Accept that some people are going to hate your writing. Here's an Amazon review of one of my books:

> **1.0 out of 5 stars Not a single likable character in this book!**
>
> **Reviewed in the United States on March 11, 2018**
>
> **It's a good thing this local guy had a few friends who were willing to write the 5-star reviews, here. Otherwise, if this book had been widely read, the ratings would more accurately reflect how terrible this thing is. The characters in it are truly gross slackers, and unlikable for being so. There's nothing funny in the book, at least in the first twenty pages, which is all I could stomach. Not Recommended!**

LOL!!!!!

Novelist DH Lawrence would take his first drafts and burn them. Literally! Then he would sit down and rewrite the book from memory...

I don't recommend that.

You probably want to save your 1st draft with a different file name, so you can always go back to it. Then, revise:

- Run through from the beginning....
- Spellcheck
- Run through all through again
- Dialogue punctuation
- Widows & Orphans (We'll talk about this Thursday)
- Weasel Words (We'll talk about this Thursday)
- Read aloud forward
- Read aloud backwards

- Beginning
- End

Think of it like any of the stories you read—in this case, listen like a writer....

I hope you don't delete anything! Your words are valuable—never delete them!

But it's not unusual to have sudden unexpected unplanned changes. It's part of the process. (Though when you're facing a deadline, an inconvenient process).

Five....

KEEP MOVING FORWARD!!!!!!!!!!!!!!!!!!!!!

and

ALL TEXTS ARE FLAWED!!!!!!!!!!!!!!!!!!!!!!!!

Write what's in your heart. That's the best genre to write in.

Sure! Show me what you've learned....

Just be consistent with the rest of the story. Present tense all the way through or past tense all the way through....

Read writers who make good dialogue. For me, the first time I noticed dialogue was when I read Hemingway's novel *The Sun Also Rises*.

Then—listen to people. How do they speak—really? Listen for patterns and accents and word choice. Then—write....

Go with passion. Go with what's in your heart.

And then make that story better. Show me what you have learned.

In workshop? Turn in as much as you can get done before the deadline. Preferably—all of it.

Similar: "Dog bites man is not a story. Man bites dog is a story."

Novelty makes the news. Tragic novelty really makes the news!

42.
Make the Story Better

WHAT'S HAPPENED TO AMERICAN NEWSPAPERS IN THE LAST twenty years is really tragic. It's bad for democracy and bad for communities.

What's really corrosive to our society—our nation, our democracy—are the big social media outfits like Facebook and Twitter, who have no other ethics beyond profit....

Yes! I would say so! It's a desert noir....

As I mentioned upthread—Billy Wilder made wonderfly dark cynical movies....

Even now, after mass shootings and other tragedies, you'll see people gather at the site and leave flowers and teddy bears and whatnot.

Copy editors. They get left out of most of the movies and shows. (An exception: Season 5 of *The Wire*). They do more than check grammar/spelling/punctuation. They have to really KNOW their community and they—at least in olden days—checked everything.

Ethics (yes, reporters had ethics (sometimes)) and editors. There was always pressure to Get it Right.

(That said, go watch *His Girl Friday*, an old movie about newspaper reporters who somewhat unethical. It's streaming on Amazon).

Arrogant and lazy and condescending....

First words out: "Where's my shotgun?"

(You're always welcome to come by zoom office hours if you want to go over your work...)

How can you make your text different and better?

Can you take it another step forward in depth and emotion?

Sure! Of course.

You can, but it's a lot of work, especially if you want to write a brand-new story.

I want you to revise the stories and poems and show me what you've learned in this class. What to revise? The stories and poems that mean something to you....

Many young writers are unaware that they are writing clichés because they haven't read enough to be able to recognize clichés.

So—read more.

No, I do not....

I make multiple passes. Most passes focus on a single aspect. The revision schedule for my last novel had 34 stages. A revision schedule for a short story would be much—shorter!

You want to make it better. If that takes drastic changes—please please please take drastic changes. (And allow yourself enough time to take/make drastic changes).

Yes! That's just what I want you to do—make the story better. Change it significantly.

Re-envision it.

If your revision makes the poem or story longer, sure.

Yep....

The bar is indeed higher for the portfolio. But if you turn in something that is the same as it was...the grade might well be lower.

Why not make the story—deeper?

My revisions are always about 30% longer than the original because I find ways to expand the text and go deeper...But other writers make their first drafts longer, and then cut....

Every writer is different. Find your own path.

We'll talk about this Thursday.

Choose the story and poems that are from your heart. Then— make them better.

(You might need to grow a bigger heart?)

I think it's possible to both be sensitive and also let the reader know what the stakes are, without being offensive. Keep working at it—you will get there!

The vision of a dead granny crawling up a leg with a knife in her teeth...Also various reptiles wading around in puddles of blood....

The director was able to really make the hallucinations work.

An argument: The Dude is happy in his life! Walter's an annoying complainer, but he's happy in his complaining. Donnie was happy, Maud's happy. They are all actually "achieving." But—the Big Lebowski is not happy, and he isn't even rich, and he's achieved nothing—he's just a big unhappy phony. So—maybe, despite his lack of apparent material success, the Dude has achieved the American Dream?

Well, it's a Dream. It's always out there—something to always reach for. Is it attainable? Maybe, for a time, for some people.

Maybe for some people, not at all, ever.

I'd suggest going back and reading Christine Granados's stories—look at the structure in them. She can teach you a lot....

Sure, Bob Dylan's an important artist—then and now. Dude won a Nobel Prize. He had a big intellectual influence on writers and other artists of that time....

Me, I would've given the Nobel Prize to Chuck Berry.

43.
Read and Understand the World

I'M NOT SURE THERE'S ANY SUPER DEEP SIGNIFICANCE—SHE'S A character who complicates the situation....

Though the 1960s were a more innocent time than many people realize....

Basically, you can either BANG or BUILD UP when you start a story—each has their advantages. For my current work in progress—the narrative needs to be LOUD and FAST....

(There are no semi-colons in the book!)

My voice was a little scratchy from teaching all day.

A very good drug-use down & out novel-in-stories is *Jesus' Son*, by Denis Johnson. But that takes place mostly in Iowa....

I just try to take it at face value—which is—this is crazy!

Yep, this weekend....

(I hope).

Ether! People indeed took it, and some still do. (See *The*

Cider House Rules, by John Irving, which has an ether-addict character). Very dangerous, though, because it is highly flammable! Don't do it! Look on YouTube for videos of comedian Richard Pryor, who set himself on fire while free-basing cocaine and ether. (Don't worry, he's not on fire in the videos, just talking about having once been on fire...).

A good story. Stories, usually, are about an individual who has a problem and might or might not try to solve the problem. Plot is not that important! Character, setting, and language are generally more important than "plot."

I'm a fiction guy, and there's more to look at in a story....

Sure, if I couldn't teach, I'd still write—I'd be a fly fishing guide who writes. Or a bureaucrat who writes. Or a hermit who writes. Something like that....

I have a hard time answering questions like this. I think our conceptions of genre are so different. For me it's fiction, non-fiction, or poetry. And—I write fiction....

My characters almost universally hate authority. They do not like being told what to do—by anyone.

(In that respect, my characters are...sort of like me!)

I don't see the things I'm interested in as repetitive...My attitude of absurdity or anger can be applied to all sorts of different things/people/situations and result in all sorts of different stories....

No Country for Old Men—excellent book and great movie.

And—a student story in the other class reminded me of *Deliverance*, a fine novel by poet James Dickey that became an excellent movie.

There are others!

The Last Picture Show, a novel by Larry McMurtry, became

an excellent film. (Take my Texas Literature class next semester and we'll read it/watch it).

In my current work in progress, there is a scene where they are hunting rats with small dogs. I wanted to play off the wolf hunt scene in Tolstoy's *War & Peace,* which is my favorite scene in that novel—and I am falling way, way short of the mark. Failing. I will make it better.

I'll fix it in revision....

I do! You see the world differently because you're trying to READ and UNDERSTAND the world....

Realistic fiction is what I grew up on and what I mostly read....

In December 1966—third grade—my parents took me to California to do Xmas with relatives. Of course we went to the beach.

And there was a guy on a jetty fly fishing, and it was the most beautiful and graceful thing I'd ever seen and have ever seen. I wanted to be like that.

(I've often wondered who that guy was—in 1966, saltwater fly fishing was pretty rare).

44.
Daylight's Burning

I SUPPOSE I'D HAVE TO CREATE A WHOLE NEW WORLD LIKE Martin or Tolkien or Jemison—but, you know what? Those would then be real worlds in my mind!

Setting isn't important because it's real—it's important because it offers space for characters to live in and move through and interact....

I think my book *Normal School* would make a good movie. *That Demon Life* would have made a good movie in the 70s—there's too much sex and bad behavior in it now to be a movie....

Are you saying each thing the best possible way you can say it? (Be honest. Are you, really?) Can you write longer sentences? Can you shift punctuation?

When writing about anyone who is not like you, you have to develop your empathy. Hang around with people who aren't like yourself. Listen to people who aren't like yourself. When writing, work at developing a person, an individual, not a stereotype.

Right now I'm reading *Intuitive Editing*, by Tiffany Martin Yates. I like it a lot, will probably use it in future classes....

Yes! You'll see new things and stories—and you'll look backwards at where you came from and see it differently....

I write to understand the world, so I approach difficult topics with—anticipation. In a practical sense—I make outlines and lists, getting closer and closer to whatever is at the center of my attention....

Keep moving forward!

All texts are flawed!

It's not the book in your head!

We'll talk about this in zoom class Thursday....

Sure!

Kim Addonizio gives prompts for that in *Ordinary Genius*. I think it would be hard to do in a story, though.

(BTW—what *does* a rock think about?)

Setting. A sense of place.

This is something really important and too often overlooked....

I think often of my first-grade teacher, Mrs. Mallet, who told us to never ever start a sentence with "and" or use "and" more than once in a sentence.

And she was wrong, and her commandment haunts me now more than 55 years later, and I still hear her voice every time I sit down to write.

(Actually, she was probably right for teaching first graders how to write, but wrong for any adult writing a novel—but we can ignore that for now).

It might be the same for cussing. The old mom admonition that "people who curse have poor vocabularies" is demonstrably not true, but it too often gets imprinted on the mind when people are young and stays with them.

And, you know, moms might have a reason to say this—potty-mouthed kids can be annoying.

But we're adults now, and we're writers, and words are all we have. Cuss words are fine. They're really fucking useful!

What we all need to do as writers is build ourselves the mind with which we want to operate in the world. We get to decide what we think and how we think.

How do you want to think?

Please don't consider revision as merely fixing mistakes. Think of it as RE-envisioning your work—seeing it in a different way and making it more true to your objective as a writer. That might not be helpful in a practical sense, but it is crucial in a moral sense.

Me? I'm looking for better writing. As simple and difficult as that. I'm looking to see what you've learned in this class....

I regret not finding a way to deal with depression and anxiety when I was young....

Totally! Everyone has gotten better—I see it in your writing practices and in your journals....

Austin Kleon has a book for that: *Keep Going: 10 Ways to Stay Creative in Good Times and Bad*

It's very helpful!

I'm not sure anything in a movie can be called random, though. Movies cost a lot to make, and everything you see on the screen is deliberate.

Dreams, by the way, are really had to do in fiction or in film.

These are great!

"Phone's ringing, Dude" is worth the price of a movie ticket all by itself.

A focus on plot rather than character—a common problem in my dedicated creative writing classes, too.

Daylight's burning.

The sand is running from the hourglass.

Time & tide wait for no one....

Our time on this Earth is ephemeral....

"Hold fast to the dreams of your youth...."

"Use well the years...."

Keep writing—keep moving forward—

Reading List

WORKS CITED, WORKS REFERENCED, WORKS PONDERED....

Abbey, Edward. *Desert Solitaire*. Touchstone, 1990.

Abbott, Megan. *Dare Me*. Media tie-in Edition, Back Bay Books, 2019.

---. *Give Me Your Hand*. Reprint edition, Back Bay Books, 2019.

---. *The Turnout*. Large type / Large print edition, Random House Large Print, 2021.

Addonizio, Kim. *Ordinary Genius: A Guide for the Poet Within*. Original edition, W. W. Norton & Company, 2009.

Alison, Jane. *Meander, Spiral, Explode: Design and Pattern in Narrative*. Catapult, 2019.

Anders, Charlie Jane. *Never Say You Can't Survive*. Tordotcom, 2021.

Aragon, Cecilia, et al. *Writers in the Secret Garden: Fanfiction, Youth, and New Forms of Mentoring.* Illustrated edition, The MIT Press, 2019.

Association, Horror Writers. *On Writing Horror: A Handbook by the Horror Writers Association.* Edited by Mort Castle, 2nd edition, Writer's Digest Books, 2006.

Bell, James Scott. *The Last Fifty Pages: The Art and Craft of Unforgettable Endings.* Compendium Press, 2019.

Bell, Matt. *Refuse to Be Done: How to Write and Rewrite a Novel in Three Drafts.* Soho Press, 2022.

Brewer, Robert Lee, editor. *Guide to Literary Agents 30th Edition: The Most Trusted Guide to Getting Published.* 30th edition, Writer's Digest Books, 2021.

Brown, Jericho. *The Tradition.* Later Printing edition, Copper Canyon Press, 2019.

Burns, Ken, and Lynn Novick. *Hemingway: A Film by Ken Burns and Lynn Novick.* PBS (Direct), 2021.

Butler, Robert Olen. *From Where You Dream: The Process of Writing Fiction.* Edited by Janet Burroway, Reprint edition, Grove Press, 2006.

Cantú, Norma Elia. *Canícula: Snapshots of a Girlhood En La Frontera, Updated Edition.* Updated ed. edition, University of New Mexico Press, 2015.

Caro, Robert A. *The Path to Power.* Vintage, 1990.

---. *Working.* Knopf, 2019.

Casares, Oscar. *Brownsville: Stories.* 1st edition, Back Bay Books, 2003.

Castro, Joy. *Flight Risk.* Lake Union Publishing, 2021.

Chávez, Denise. *The Last of the Menu Girls.* Reprint edition,

Vintage, 2004.

---. *Loving Pedro Infante*. Washington Square Press, 2002.

Chavez, Felicia Rose. *The Anti-Racist Writing Workshop: How To Decolonize the Creative Classroom*. Haymarket Books, 2021.

Clancy, Tom. *The Hunt for Red October*. Reprint edition, Berkley, 2010.

Cleave, Ryan Van. *Memoir Writing For Dummies*. 1st edition, For Dummies, 2013.

Coen, Joel. *The Big Lebowski*. Universal Pictures Home Entertainment, 2009.

Coppola, Francis Ford. *The Godfather Notebook*. Reprint edition, Regan Arts., 2016.

Crook, Elizabeth. *The Which Way Tree*. Back Bay Books, 2019.

Dickey, James. *Deliverance*. Reprint edition, Delta, 1994.

Diners, Drive-Ins & Dives: The Complete Fourth Season. MILLENIUM MEDIA SEVICES, 2010.

Dobie, J. Frank. *Tales of Old-Time Texas*. Reprint edition, University of Texas Press, 1984.

Dora, Liza. *Is Lena Pretty?* Edited by Jolie Gray, Illustrated edition, Liza Dora, 2015.

Dreyer, Benjamin. *Dreyer's English: An Utterly Correct Guide to Clarity and Style*. Reprint edition, Random House Trade Paperbacks, 2020.

Eastwood, Clint. *Fistful of Dollars*. Metro Goldwyn Mayer, 2008.

Ellis, Sherry. *Now Write!: Fiction Writing Exercises from

Today's Best Writers and Teachers. Later Printing Edition, TarcherPerigee, 2006.

Everett, Percival. *Damned If I Do: Stories.* First Paperback Edition, Graywolf Press, 2004.

---. *Half an Inch of Water: Stories.* 1st Edition, Graywolf Press, 2015.

---. *Watershed.* 2nd edition, Beacon Press, 2003.

Fitzgerald, F. Scott. *The Great Gatsby.* Scribners, 2003.

Flaherty, Alice. *The Midnight Disease: The Drive to Write, Writer's Block, and the Creative Brain.* Houghton Mifflin, 2004.

Fontenot, Rebecca. *No Such Thing as Feeling Young.* Independently published, 2021.

Ford, John, et al. *The Searchers.* 2019.

Forster, E. M. *Aspects of the Novel.* New York: Harcourt Brace Jovanovich, 1954.

French, Tana. *The Searcher.* Penguin Books, 2020.

---. *The Witch Elm.* Penguin Books, 2019.

Gaines, Ernest J. *A Lesson Before Dying.* Vintage, 1994.

---. *A Long Day in November.* Reissue edition, Lizzie Skurnick Books, 2013.

---. *Bloodline.* W W Norton & Co Inc, 1976.

Gardner, John. *The Art of Fiction.* New York: Knopf, 1984.

---. *On Becoming a Novelist.* New York: Harper & Row, 1983.

Gay, Roxane. *Ayiti.* Later Printing edition, Grove Press, 2018.

---. "Not Here to Make Friends." *BuzzFeed,* https://www.

buzzfeed.com/roxanegay/not-here-to-make-friends-unlikable. Accessed 13 Nov. 2021.

Givhan, Jennifer. *Trinity Sight*. 2019.

Goetzmann, William H. *Army Exploration in the American West, 1803-1863*. Univ. of Nebraska Press, 1979.

Goetzmann, William H., and William N. Goetzmann. *The West of the Imagination*. Second edition, University of Oklahoma Press, 2009.

Gran, Sara. *Claire DeWitt and the Bohemian Highway*. Reprint edition, Mariner Books, 2014.

---. *Claire DeWitt and the City of the Dead*. Reprint edition, Mariner Books, 2012.

---. *Come Closer*. Soho Press, 2011.

---. *The Infinite Blacktop*. Reprint edition, Washington Square Press, 2019.

Granados, Christine. *Brides and Sinners in El Chuco: Short Stories*. University of Arizona Press, 2006.

---. *Fight Like a Man and Other Stories We Tell Our Children*. First Edition, University of New Mexico Press, 2017.

Hall-Wilson, Lisa. *Method Acting For Writers: Learn Deep Point Of View Using Emotional Layers*. Lisa Hall-Wilson, 2018.

Hand, Elizabeth. *Generation Loss*. Small Beer Press, 2020.

---. *The Book of Lamps and Banners*. Mulholland Books, 2020.

Harrison, Jim. *The Shape of the Journey: New & Collected Poems*. Reprint edition, Copper Canyon Press, 2000.

---. *The Woman Lit by Fireflies*. Reprint edition, Grove Press, 2008.

Hawks, Howard. *His Girl Friday*. Criterion Collection, 2017.

Hearon, Shelby. *A Prince of a Fellow*. Doubleday, 1978.

Heinemann, Larry. *Paco's Story*. Farrar Straus Giroux, 1986.

Hemingway, Ernest. *For Whom the Bell Tolls*. Scribner, 1995.

---. *The Complete Short Stories of Ernest Hemingway: The Finca Vigia Edition*. The Finca Vigia Edition, Scribner, 1998.

---. *The Sun Also Rises: The Hemingway Library Edition*. Hemingway Library ed. edition, Scribner, 2016.

Hills, L. Rust. *Writing in General and the Short Story in Particular*. Boston: Houghton Mifflin, 2000.

Hugo, Richard. *The Triggering Town: Lectures and Essays on Poetry and Writing*. Reissue edition, W. W. Norton & Company, 2010.

Huns, The. "Glad He's Dead." https://www.youtube.com/watch?v=pj98pr2DbSo.

Hynes, James. *Kings of Infinite Space*. First edition, Picador, 2005.

Iglesias, Gabino. *Coyote Songs*. Broken River Books, 2018.

---. *The Devil Brings You Home*. Mulholland Books, 2023.

Irving, John. *The Cider House Rules*. Later Printing edition, Ballantine Books, 1997.

---. *A Prayer for Owen Meany: A Novel*. Mariner Books Reprint, 2012.

Jeffers, Honorée Fanonne. *The Age of Phillis*. Wesleyan University Press, 2022.

---. *The Love Songs of W.E.B. Du Bois: An Oprah's Book Club Novel*. 1st Edition, Harper, 2021.

Jemisin, N. K. *The Fifth Season*. Orbit, 2015.

---. *The Obelisk Gate*. Reprint edition, Orbit, 2016.

---. *The Stone Sky*. Reprint edition, Orbit, 2017.

Johnson, Denis. *Jesus' Son*. Methuen Pub Ltd, 2004.

Johnston, Antony. *The Organised Writer: How to Stay on Top of All Your Projects and Never Miss a Deadline*. Bloomsbury Yearbooks, 2020.

Jones, Amy, editor. *Novel & Short Story Writer's Market 40th Edition: The Most Trusted Guide to Getting Published*. 40th edition, Writer's Digest Books, 2021

Judge, Mike, et al. *Office space*. 2019.

King, Stephen. *It*. Media Tie-In edition, Scribner, 2019.

---. *On Writing*. New York: Scribner, 2010.

Kleon, Austin. *Keep Going: 10 Ways to Stay Creative in Good Times and Bad*. Illustrated edition, Workman Publishing Company, 2019.

---. *Show Your Work!: 10 Ways to Share Your Creativity and Get Discovered*. Illustrated edition, Workman Publishing, 2014.

---. *Steal Like an Artist: 10 Things Nobody Told You About Being Creative*. 1st edition, Workman Publishing, 2012.

Kohn, Alfie. *Ungrading: Why Rating Students Undermines Learning*. Edited by Susan D. Blum, 1st edition, West Virginia University Press, 2020.

Kurosawa, Akira, et al. *Yojimbo*. Criterion Collection, 2007.

Lamott, Anne. *Bird by Bird: Some Instructions on Writing*

and Life. First Printing Thus edition, Anchor, 1995.

Leonard, Elmore. *Rum Punch*. Reprint edition, William Morrow Paperbacks, 2011.

Locke, Attica. *Black Water Rising*. Harper Perennial ed. edition, Amistad, 2010.

---. *Bluebird, Bluebird*. Reprint edition, Mulholland Books, 2018.

---. *Heaven, My Home*. Mulholland Books, 2020.

Madis, McKenna. *Letters: I'll Never Send*. Independently published, 2021.

Martin, George R. R. *A Game of Thrones*. New York: Bantam, 1996.

---. *A Clash of Kings*. New York: Bantam, 1999.

---. *A Storm of Swords*. New York: Bantam, 2000.

---. *A Feast for Crows*. New York: Bantam, 2005.

---. *A Dance with Dragons*. New York: Bantam, 2011

Martin, Tiffany Yates. *Intuitive Editing: A Creative and Practical Guide to Revising Your Writing*. E3 Press, 2020.

Matejka, Adrian. *Somebody Else Sold the World*. Penguin Books, 2021.

---. *The Big Smoke*. 1st edition, Penguin Books, 2013.

Matthews, Aaron, et al. *The War and Peace of Tim O'Brien*. 2020.

McCarthy, Cormac. *Blood Meridian: Or the Evening Redness in the West*. Knopf Doubleday Publishing Group, 1992.

---. *The Road*. Knopf Doubleday Publishing Group, 2006.

McMurtry, Larry. *Lonesome Dove*. Simon & Schuster Paperbacks, 2010.

---. *The Last Picture Show*. Reprint edition, Liveright, 2018.

Melville, Herman. *Moby-Dick, or The Whale*. Penguin Classics, Paperback, 2002.

Michener, James A. *Hawaii*. Reprint edition, Dial Press Trade Paperback, 2002.

Nash, Jennie. *Blueprint for a Book: Build Your Novel from the Inside Out*. Tree Farm Books, 2021.

Oates, Joyce Carol. *The Doll-Master and Other Tales of Terror*. Reprint edition, Mysterious Press, 2017.

---. *Zombie*. Illustrated edition, Ecco, 2009.

O'Connor, Flannery. *The Complete Stories*. First edition, Farrar, Straus and Giroux, 1971.

---. *Mystery and Manners*. New York: Farrar, Straus & Giroux, 1969.

Oliver, Mary. *A Poetry Handbook*. First edition, Mariner Books, 1994.

Peña, Daniel. *Bang*. Arte Publico Press, 2018.

Percy, Benjamin. *Thrill Me: Essays on Fiction*. Minneapolis: Graywolf, 2016.

Polanski, Roman, et al. *Chinatown:* [DVD][videorecording. 2017.

Pryor, Richard. *Richard Pryor Live on Sunset Strip*. Sony Pictures Home Entertainment, 2006.

Pushkin, Alexander. *Eugene Onegin*. Translated by Stanley Mitchell, 1st edition, Penguin Classics, 2008.

Pushkin, Alexander, and John Bayley. *Tales of Belkin and Other Prose Writings*. Translated by Ronald Wilks, 1st edition, Penguin Classics, 1998.

Reeb, Annabeth. *Howdy's Adventures in Aggieland*. Mascot Kids, 2021.

Reeves, Roger. *King Me*. Copper Canyon Press, 2013.

Rowell, Charles H. *Making Callaloo: 25 Years of Black Literature, 1976-2000*. St. Martin's Press, 2002.

Salesses, Matthew. *Craft in the Real World: Rethinking Fiction Writing and Workshopping*. Catapult, 2021.

Saunders, George. *A Swim in a Pond in the Rain: In Which Four Russians Give a Master Class on Writing, Reading, and Life*. Random House, 2021.

Sayles, John, et al. *Lone star*. 2016.

See, Carolyn. *Making a Literary Life: Advice for Writers and Other Dreamers*. New York: Random House, 2003.

Shelnutt, Eve. *Writing: The Translation of Memory*. New York: MacMillan,1990.

Shulman, Leigh. *The Writer's Roadmap: Paving the Way to Your Ideal Writing Life*. Future Is Red, The, 2018.

Singleton, George. *Pep Talks, Warnings & Screeds: Indispensable Wisdom and Cautionary Advice for Writers* / Wallace, Daniel, ; Illustrator. Writer's Digest Books, 2008.

Smith, Patti. *Just Kids*. 1st edition, Ecco, 2010.

Solzhenitsyn, Alexander. *August 1914*. Translated by H. T. Willetts, Penguin Books, 1992.

Some Wayne State Professors Still Pushing to Teach Remotely – *The Wayne Stater*. https://thewaynestater.

com/20647/news/some-wayne-state-professors-still-pushing-to-teach-remotely/#. Accessed 12 Nov. 2021.

Stevens, George, et al. *Giant*. 2020.

The Clash. *London Calling*. Epic, 2000.

The Sopranos - The Complete Series 2007. Warner Home Video, 2009.

Tolkien, J. R. R. *The Fellowship of the Ring: Being the First Part of The Lord of the Rings*. Illustrated edition, Mariner Books, 2012.

---. *The Return of the King: Being the Third Part of the Lord of the Rings*. Illustrated edition, Mariner Books, 2012.

---. *The Silmarillion*. HarperCollins, 1991

---. *The Two Towers: Being the Second Part of The Lord of the Rings*. Illustrated edition, Mariner Books, 2012.

Tolstoy, Leo, and Orlando Figes. *War and Peace*. Translated by Anthony Briggs, Deluxe edition, Penguin Classics, 2006.

Toole, John Kennedy, and Walker Percy. *A Confederacy of Dunces*. 20th Anniversary ed. edition, Grove Weidenfeld, 1987.

Ueland, Brenda, and Andrei Codrescu. *If You Want to Write: A Book about Art, Independence and Spirit*. 2nd edition, Graywolf Press, 2007.

van der Kolk, Bessel. *The Body Keeps the Score: Brain, Mind, and Body in the Healing of Trauma*. Reprint edition, Penguin Publishing Group, 2015.

Various. *The Wire: The Complete Series*. HBO Studios, 2011.

Waggoner, Tim. *Writing in the Dark*. Illustrated edition, Guide Dog Books, 2020.

Walker, Rob. *The Art of Noticing: 131 Ways to Spark Creativity, Find Inspiration, and Discover Joy in the Everyday.* Illustrated edition, Knopf, 2019.

Welty, Eudora. *One Writer's Beginnings.* Boston: Faber & Faber, 1984

Wetmore, Elizabeth. *Valentine.* 2021.

White, Lowell Mick. *Burnt House.* Buffalo Times Press, 2018.

---. *Long Time Ago Good.* Buffalo Times Press, 2016.

---. *Normal School.* Buffalo Times Press, 2019.

---. *Professed: A Novel of Higher Education.* Buffalo Times Press, 2016.

---. *That Demon Life.* 1st edition, Gival Press, LLC, 2009.

---. *The Messes We Make of Our Lives: Stories.* Buffalo Times Press, 2017.

Wilder, Billy. *Ace in the Hole.* Criterion Collection, 2018.

Willis, Bruce, et al. *Last man standing.* Warner Home Video, 2010.

Wolfe, Tom. *The Right Stuff.* Second Edition, Revised, Picador, 2008.

---. *The Bonfire of the Vanities.* First edition, Picador, 2008.

Acknowledgements

A SPECIAL LEVEL OF GRATITUDE AND APPRECIATION GOES TO the Young Scholars who've inhabited my classrooms these past however many years, for paying attention when it was important to pay attention and for mostly working hard at their writing. And more thanks to Texas A&M University, for paying me to do some interesting and useful things. And even more thanks to all the many good writers and critics and citizens and friends who provided advice and help and encouragement along the way: Andrea Bates, Patricia Bjorklund, Pamela Booton, Florence Davies, Ken Fontenot, Deven Green, Jason Harris, Alysa Hayes, Wende Hilsenrod, Anne Goetzmann Kelley, Kathryn Lane, Erika Liesman, Amira Mazzawy, Moon Set-Byul, Teri Sink, Reji Thomas, Javier Booton, Stella Wilde, Diane Wilson.

About Lowell Mick White

LOWELL MICK WHITE IS THE AUTHOR OF SIX PREVIOUS BOOKS: novels *Normal School* and *Professed* and *Burnt House* and *That Demon Life,* and story collections *Long Time Ago Good* and *The Messes We Make of Our Lives.* A winner of the Dobie-Paisano Fellowship and a member of the Texas Institute of Letters, White received his PhD from Texas A&M University.

Contact Lowell Mick White at www.lowellmickwhite.com

www.ingramcontent.com/pod-product-compliance
Lightning Source LLC
Chambersburg PA
CBHW060523080526
44586CB00012B/596